Technical Analysis Mastery

The Sniper Trader's Guide to Price Action, Chart Patterns & Market Psychology

Tabraz Ahmed

notionpress.com

INDIA • SINGAPORE • MALAYSIA

ISBN

Hardcase 979-8-90392-561-2
Paperback 979-8-90392-560-5

Technical Analysis Mastery:
The Sniper's Guide to Dominating the Markets

By Tabraz Ahmed

"In trading, patience is power, discipline is your weapon, and technical mastery is your ultimate shield." 🎯

🙏

Dedication

This book is dedicated to all the aspiring traders who dare to master their craft with precision and patience.

To those who understand that in the markets — it's not about fighting, but about flowing with intelligence.

May you find your sniper focus, your trading edge, and your freedom.

✍

Author's Note

Trading is often misunderstood.
People chase magical indicators, secret formulas, and quick wins — only to realize that the true path is very different.

Master traders don't gamble.
They study.
They observe.
They act with sniper-like precision.

This book was born from the idea that anyone — yes, *anyone* — can learn the art of technical analysis if it's explained simply, step-by-step, and backed by real examples.

I wrote this not as a guru.
Not as a market predictor.
But as a fellow learner who believes that trading is 80% psychology, 20% technique — and 100% discipline.

Wherever you are in your trading journey — beginner, intermediate, or returning warrior —
this book will serve as your guide, your shield, and your silent mentor.

Now, breathe deep.
Focus your scope.
It's time to become a sniper in the markets.

– Tabraz Ahmed

Table of Contents

Chapter 1

What is Technical Analysis Really About?

✍ Introduction:

A Calm Conversation with the Markets

In a world full of noise, news, predictions, and endless opinions, there exists one quiet truth: **price.**

Price doesn't shout.
It doesn't beg for your attention.
It simply moves — up, down, sideways — reflecting every emotion, every belief, every fear in the market at that moment.

Technical Analysis is the art of listening to that quiet truth.

It is not about fortune-telling.
It is not about guessing tomorrow's newspaper headline.
It's about **observing how price behaves right now** and **aligning yourself smartly** with the flow of the market.

A professional trader is like a surfer.
He doesn't create the waves.
He reads them — patiently, carefully, with respect.
And when the right wave comes, he rides it gracefully.
This book will teach you to become that surfer.
That sniper.
That silent professional who moves with the market, not against it.

🧠 What Technical Analysis Really Means

Let's destroy the first big misunderstanding right now:
Technical Analysis does NOT predict the future.

Instead, it studies what price is doing in the present —
and offers you a way to make intelligent, probability-based decisions.

When you master technical analysis, you are not trying to guess what will happen next.
You are positioning yourself smartly, saying:
"If this pattern appears,
If this level holds,
If this volume spikes,
Then I will act."

You move based on **evidence**, not **emotion**.
You become a scientist of the market — calm, methodical, patient.

📖 A Short Story: The Chessboard and The Ocean

Imagine two people trying to navigate a vast ocean.

The first believes he can control the waves.
He shouts orders at the sea, demands it to behave, and gets angry when storms come.

The second accepts that he cannot control the ocean.
Instead, he studies the tides, the wind patterns, the behavior of waves.
He learns when to move, when to wait, when to attack.

The second man survives.
The second man thrives.

Technical Analysis makes you the second man.

The market is the ocean.
Your charts are your map.
Your technical knowledge is your compass.

📈 Why Price Matters More Than News

Every opinion in the world eventually shows up in one place: the price chart.

If a company announces record profits but the stock falls,
price is telling you the real story — not the headlines.

If economic data comes in worse than expected, but the index rallies,
price is telling you where the real power lies.

In the end, price is pure.
Price is unfiltered reality.
Price is the truth.

Learn to listen to it.
And you'll be free from the noise forever.

🧠 The Three Core Skills of a Technical Trader

To master technical analysis, you must develop three critical skills:

1. **Observation**

   Calmly watching price behavior without bias.
   Seeing the patterns, the reactions, the way price breathes.

2. **Alignment**

   Aligning yourself with the dominant market force —
   Trading with the trend, not against it.

3. **Execution**

   Acting precisely when your plan tells you to.
   Not earlier. Not later.
   Just right.

These three skills form the heart of every great trader.

Master them, and you are already ahead of 90% of the market.

Technical Trading Cycle

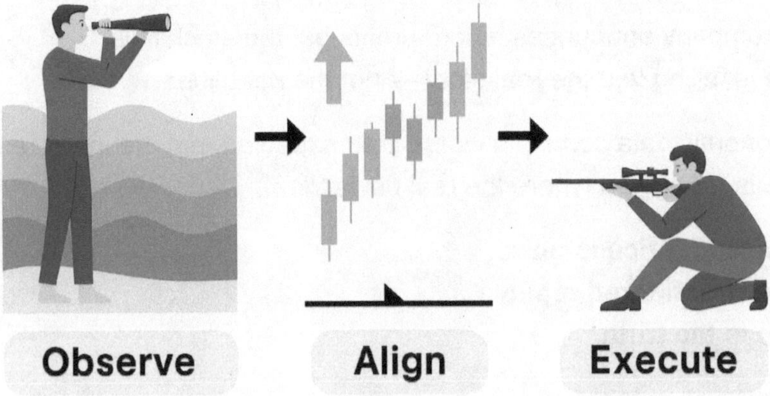

🔥 Real Example: The Nifty Breakout Whisper

In March 2025, Nifty 50 hovered between 22,300 and 22,450 for almost a week.

- Price was quiet.
- Volume was low.
- Traders were bored, anxious, impatient.

Then one Friday afternoon, something changed:

- A large bullish candle closed firmly above 22,450.
- Volume spiked higher than any day that week.

Technical traders didn't need breaking news.
They didn't need insider tips.

They could **see** the market's language:
Buyers had silently overwhelmed the sellers.

A sniper trader, watching patiently, aligned himself with the breakout and entered.
Within 48 hours, Nifty rallied over 250 points.

No prediction.
Just observation, alignment, and clean execution.

That is the power of true technical analysis.

🛡 Protecting Yourself: Why Risk Management Comes First

Technical Analysis doesn't guarantee profits.
It only gives you **high-probability opportunities**.

Every professional trader knows:

> "It's not about how much you win.
> It's about how well you manage when you lose."

Because even the best setups sometimes fail.
Even the most beautiful breakouts sometimes reverse.

That's why **Risk Management** is the hidden backbone of every technical strategy.

In future chapters, we'll go deep into:

- How to size your trades
- How to place your stops
- How to protect your capital like a true professional

But for now, remember:
Risk Management is your shield.
Technical Analysis is your sword.

Both are necessary for survival and success.

🎯 Chapter 1: Key Takeaways

- Price is the only truth that matters.
- Technical Analysis reads the present, not predicts the future.
- Great traders master **Observation → Alignment → Execution**.
- Protecting your capital is even more important than finding winning setups.

🧘 Final Mentor Tip:

The market doesn't owe you anything.
It doesn't reward hope.
It rewards preparation, discipline, and emotional strength.

Become the calm professional.
Become the patient sniper.
Become the master surfer of the market's waves.

🎯

Chapter 2

Candlesticks — The Language of Price Action

✍ Introduction:

A Market Conversation Without Words

Imagine two armies facing each other on a battlefield.
Neither side speaks.
Neither side shows their plans.
Yet every small movement — a step forward, a shield raised, a sudden retreat —
gives away their intentions.

Candlesticks are the silent movements of the market armies.

Each candle is a footprint —
a mark left by the ongoing battle between buyers and sellers.

Learn to read these footprints,
and you will understand who is winning, who is losing, and when the tides are about to turn.

Candlesticks are not magic.
They are human behavior made visible.

Greed, fear, hesitation, aggression — all of it is captured inside a simple candle.

Master candlesticks, and you master the language of price.

☑ The Heartbeat of a Candle: Open, High, Low, Close

Every candlestick represents a small story told over a specific time period —
5 minutes, 15 minutes, 1 hour, 1 day — depending on your chart.

The candle records four critical moments:

- **Open:** Where the story began
- **High:** The most aggressive point for buyers
- **Low:** The deepest counterattack by sellers
- **Close:** Where the battle finally ended

These four points create a complete emotional map of that timeframe.

When you learn to interpret this map,
you no longer guess — you *know* who had the advantage.

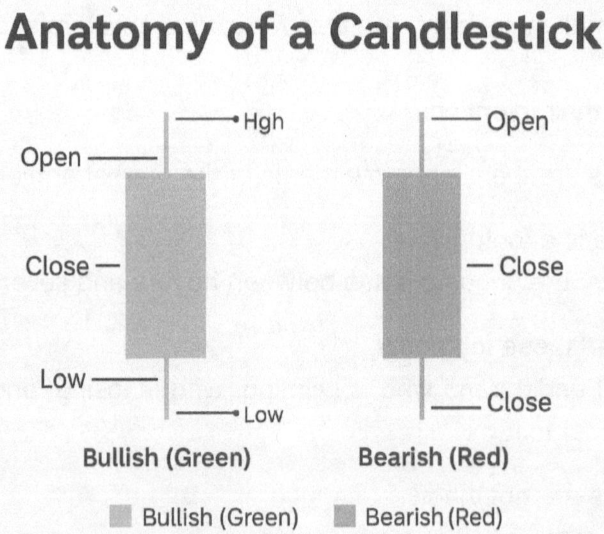

🧠 Bullish vs Bearish Candles: The Silent Emotions

- A **Bullish Candle** tells you buyers dominated.
  The close is above the open.
  Momentum favors upside.
- A **Bearish Candle** tells you sellers controlled the fight.
  The close is below the open.
  Momentum leans downward.

But it's not just about color.
It's about **how much** they dominated, **where** they dominated, and **when** they dominated.

A tiny bullish candle in the middle of nowhere?
Not powerful.

A giant bullish candle breaking resistance after long consolidation?
That's a sniper signal.

The candle's size, wick length, and context matter massively.

📚 Reading a Candle Like a Master

Whenever you see a candle, ask these three questions:

1. **Where did it open?**
2. **Where did it close?**
3. **Did price face rejection (wicks)?**

👉 A long upper wick?
Sellers slammed the door on buyers.

👉 A long lower wick?
Buyers defended the battlefield after heavy selling.

👉 No wicks, just a full body?
One side dominated completely.

Candlesticks are mini psychological battles made visual.

You must learn to read their mood, their strength, their hesitation.

🛡 Key Candlestick Signals

While there are dozens of patterns, a few stand out because they consistently reveal shifts in power:

◍ The Hammer

A candle with:

- A small body near the top
- A long lower wick

It appears after a decline —
and signals that sellers attacked hard but buyers smashed back before closing.

It whispers: "The worst is over. Strength is returning."

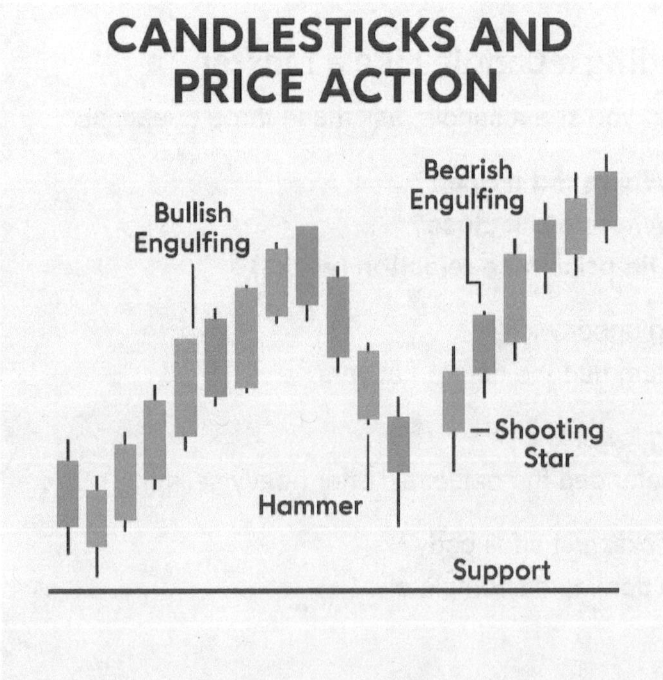

◍ The Bullish Engulfing

Two candles:

- First a red candle (sellers winning)
- Then a large green candle fully "eats" the previous red one

It signals a major momentum shift —
buyers overwhelmed the sellers completely.

It's like a wounded army suddenly rallying and pushing back with full force.

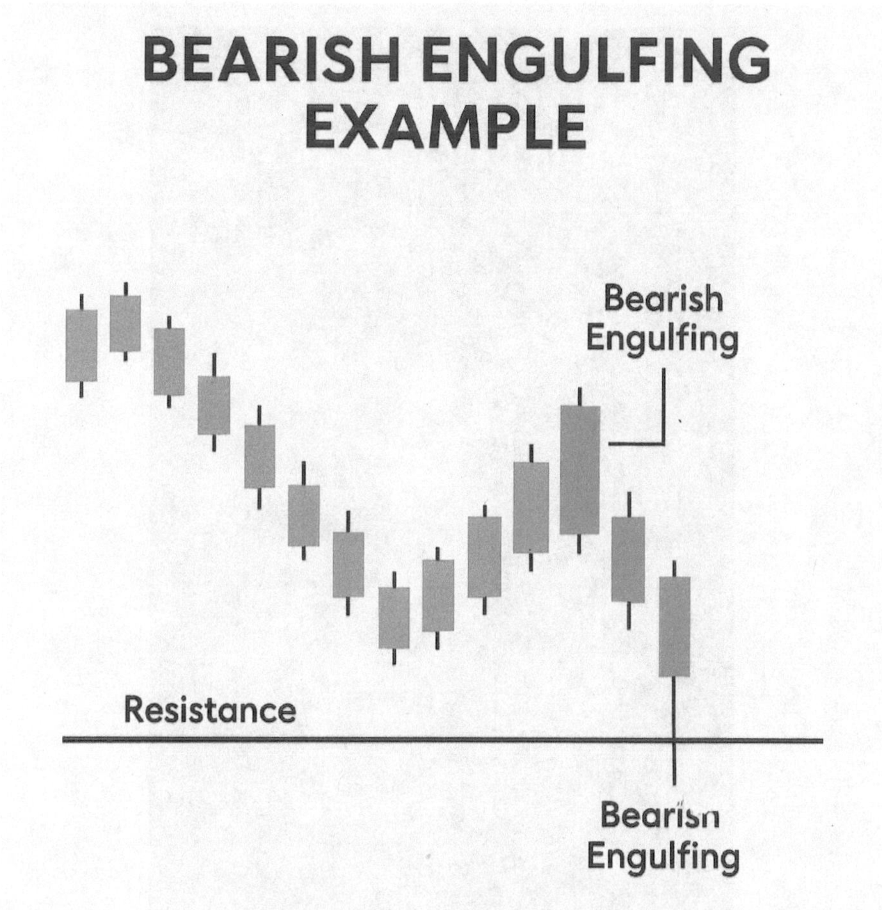

● The Shooting Star

A candle with:

- Small body near the bottom
- Long upper wick

Appears after an uptrend.
It means buyers tried pushing higher but were brutally rejected by sellers.

A sniper sees a shooting star at resistance —
and knows the tide may be turning.

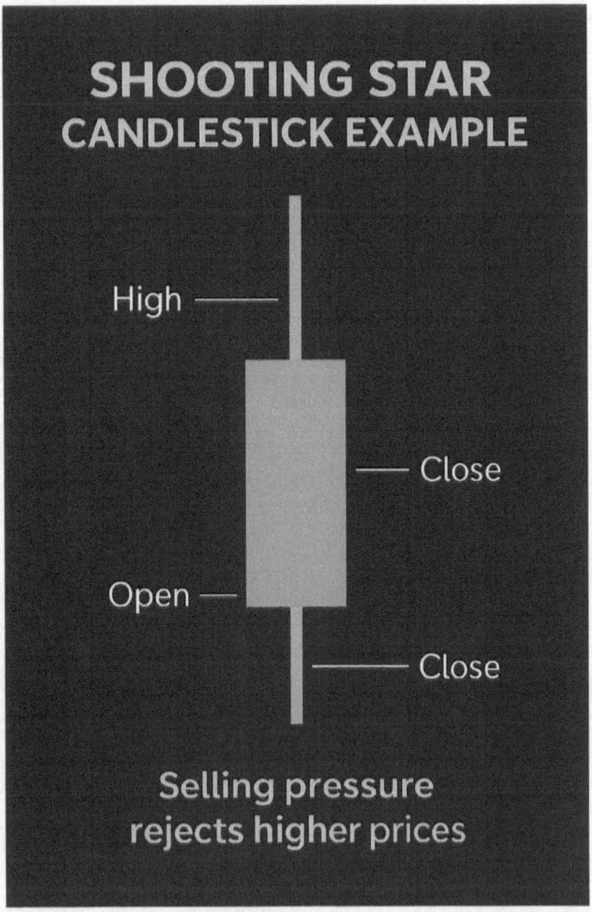

🧠 Candlestick Psychology is King

Don't just memorize patterns.
Understand why they form.

A Hammer is not just a green candle.
It's **buyer exhaustion reversing** into **buyer aggression**.

A Shooting Star is not just a red candle.
It's **buyer greed getting crushed by overwhelming sell pressure**.

When you feel the emotional battle behind the candles,
you become a true market reader — not just a pattern scanner.

💰 Real Example: BankNifty Shooting Star Reversal

BankNifty was rallying hard towards 48,500.
Momentum was strong.
Everyone was bullish.

Then suddenly on the 15-min chart:

- A perfect Shooting Star appeared at resistance
- Volume spiked unusually high

Smart traders smelled the trap.
Instead of chasing higher, they prepared for reversal.

Within 2 hours, BankNifty dropped nearly 400 points.

No magic.
Just reading candlestick emotions in real-time.

🎯 Chapter 2: Action Plan

✅ Open TradingView or your broker chart.

✅ Look for:

- 2 examples of a Hammer after a fall
- 2 examples of a Shooting Star after a rally

✅ Screenshot them.

✅ Note the support/resistance levels.

✅ Train your eye daily for 7 days.

Recognizing these key candlesticks must become automatic — sniper reflex level.

🧘 Final Mentor Tip:

Patterns don't create profits.
Your ability to read patterns in the right place at the right time does.

The market rewards the trained observer,
not the impulsive gambler.

Master the language of candlesticks,
and you will no longer need noisy opinions ever again.

Chapter 3

Chart Patterns Simplified — Patterns That Matter

✍ Introduction:

"The Market Leaves Clues — You Just Have to Learn Their Language."

Imagine trying to track an animal through a forest.
You can't see the animal — but you can spot its footprints, its broken twigs, the crushed grass.
Each little sign tells you:

> "It was here. It moved this way. It's resting there."

In trading, **chart patterns** are those clues.

They are **the footprints of large traders, smart money, emotional waves**.
And if you learn to read them calmly,
you stop chasing noise —
you start **anticipating moves like a pro**.

This chapter is about **simplifying** chart patterns,
so you recognize what actually matters —
and ignore the endless "pattern names" thrown around on Instagram.

🧠 What Chart Patterns Really Represent

Forget the names for a second — flags, triangles, cups.

At the core, all chart patterns are about **one thing**:

Who is winning the emotional battle — buyers or sellers?

When you see a pattern forming,
you are not seeing lines and shapes.
You are watching **pressure build up**.
You are sensing **fear, greed, hesitation, and explosion points**.

The patterns are simply the result of human emotion repeating itself again... and again... and again.

📖 Story: The Coiled Spring

Imagine pressing down on a coiled spring with your hand.

At first, it resists gently.
Then, the more you press, the more pressure builds up underneath.
You can feel the tension.

At some point, the spring doesn't just rise slowly.
It **explodes upward** the moment you lift your hand.

Chart patterns work exactly like that.

- Tight consolidations = Pressure building
- Breakouts = Explosion of trapped energy

Your job as a trader is not to predict when.
Your job is to observe the spring building — and be ready when it snaps.

🧩 The Only 3 Categories of Chart Patterns You Need

Instead of memorizing 50 names,
just master these **3 basic emotional structures**:

1. Continuation Patterns — "The Trend is Pausing, Not Ending."

- Examples: Flags, Pennants, Triangles
- Meaning: Strong trend, minor cooling off, trend resumes
- Psychology: Buyers/sellers are just catching their breath, not quitting

📒 Example:
Nifty rallies from 22,000 to 22,450, then goes sideways for a few hours forming a tight triangle.
Volume dries up.
Suddenly, breakout — and next leg higher towards 22,700.

The smart trader sees the pause — not panic.
The fool thinks "top is in" — and gets shorted into the breakout.

2. Reversal Patterns — "The Battle is Changing Sides."

- Examples: Double Top, Double Bottom, Head and Shoulders
- Meaning: Trend weakening, possible turn ahead
- Psychology: Winners are getting tired, losers are regrouping

🗄 Example:
BankNifty rallies towards 49,000, forms a Double Top —
then collapses below neckline support with heavy volume.

The pattern wasn't magic.
It was simply the visible **fatigue of buyers** — and the return of seller aggression.

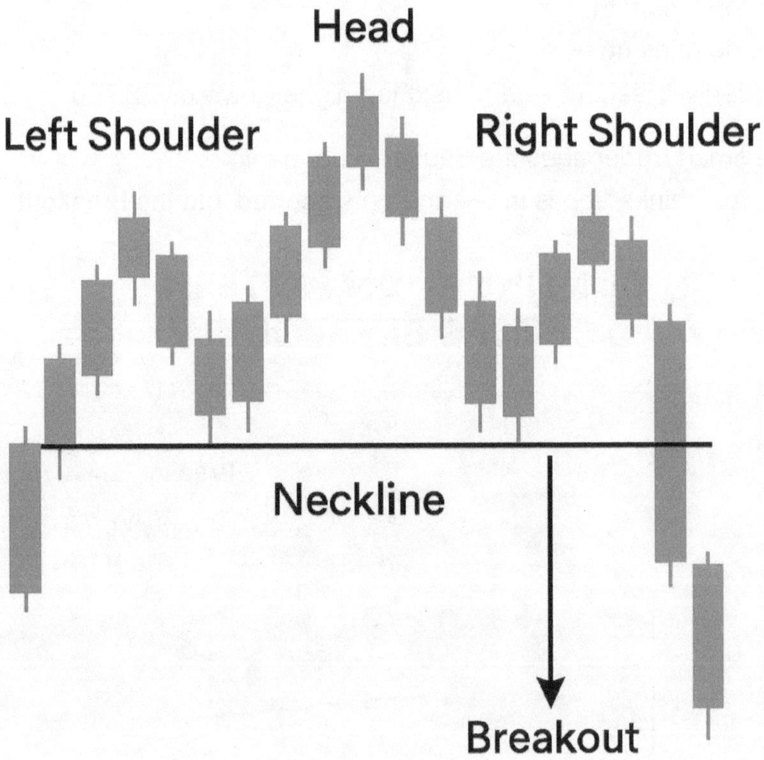

3. Bilateral Patterns — "It Could Go Either Way, Watch Carefully."

- Examples: Symmetrical Triangle, Wedges
- Meaning: Both sides fighting hard, no clear winner yet
- Psychology: Massive tug-of-war building up

📚 Example:
Tata Motors oscillates inside a Symmetrical Triangle for days.
Neither bulls nor bears dominate.
Finally, a massive breakout occurs — and whichever side wins, the move is violent.

The smart trader waits — sniper rifle ready — for the breakout confirmation.

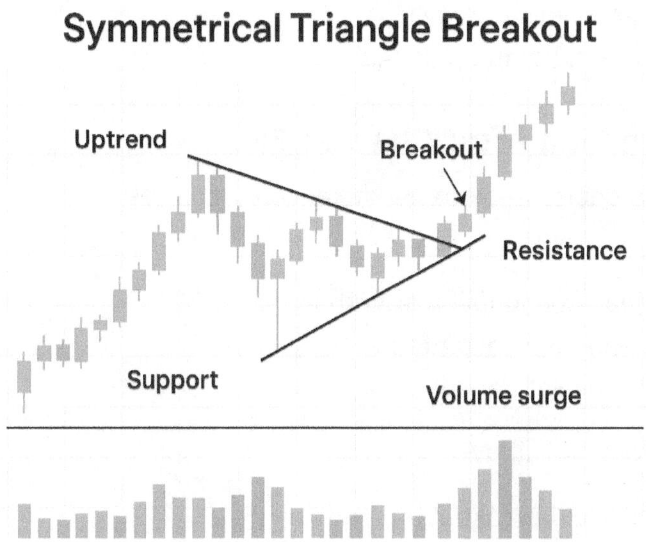

🧠 Golden Rule: The Pattern is Secondary. The Breakout Matters More.

You can draw the cleanest triangle or head and shoulders.
But until price **breaks** — the pattern means nothing.

Sniper traders are patient.
They:

- Recognize the pattern
- Mark the key breakout levels
- Wait for clean volume + candle confirmation before striking

The setup is born when the breakout happens — not before.

🛑 Rookie Mistake to Avoid

❌ Guessing breakout direction too early.
❌ Trading inside the pattern (noise = fakeouts).
❌ Ignoring volume during the breakout.

Patterns are potential energy.
Breakouts are kinetic energy.
Trade the kinetic, not the potential.

🎯 Action Plan After Chapter 3:

✅ Open 50 charts — stocks, indexes, commodities.
✅ Identify:

- 3 clean continuation patterns
- 3 clean reversal patterns
- 2 clean bilateral patterns

✅ Mark them and study:

- Where did breakout happen?
- What did volume do?
- What kind of candle closed the breakout?

✅ Build your Chart Pattern Memory.

The more patterns your brain catalogs naturally,
the faster you'll spot sniper setups in real-time.

🧘 Final Mentor Tip:

Chart patterns are not magic spells.
They are the visible scars and emotions of market battles.

Learn to see patterns as pressure points —
and you will trade **ahead of the crowd**,
while others are still guessing which name it is.

In the end, the market doesn't care if you know the difference between a wedge and a flag.
It only cares if you can read pressure correctly... and strike decisively.

Chapter 4

Trends — Riding the Big Waves

✍ Introduction:

"Why Fight the Ocean When You Can Surf It?"

Picture yourself standing at the edge of the ocean.

The waves are coming in — strong, wild, unstoppable.

You have two choices:

- Fight the waves with pure ego and get thrown around like a rag doll.
- Or learn to move **with** the waves, catching their rhythm and riding them effortlessly.

Most new traders?
They fight.
They yell at charts.
They try to short strong uptrends because "it's gone up too much!"
Or they try to buy crashing stocks because "it's too cheap now!"

Experienced traders?
They surf.
They observe.
They ride the natural trend — and let the market do the heavy lifting.

Welcome to the art of riding trends.

☑ What Exactly is a Trend?

A **trend** is simply the market's way of showing dominant emotion over time.

- **Uptrend:** Optimism and Greed win.
  Price makes **higher highs and higher lows**.
  Traders feel like rockstars.
- **Downtrend:** Fear and Panic take over.
  Price makes **lower highs and lower lows**.
  Traders suddenly start googling "best work from home jobs."
- **Sideways:** Confusion reigns.
  Price moves between support and resistance.
  Traders sit bored, questioning their life decisions, scrolling through memes while Nifty moves 3 points an hour.

✅ A trend is not magic.
✅ It's just mass emotion printed over time.

If you learn to read this flow, you stop being surprised —
and start surfing these waves with power.

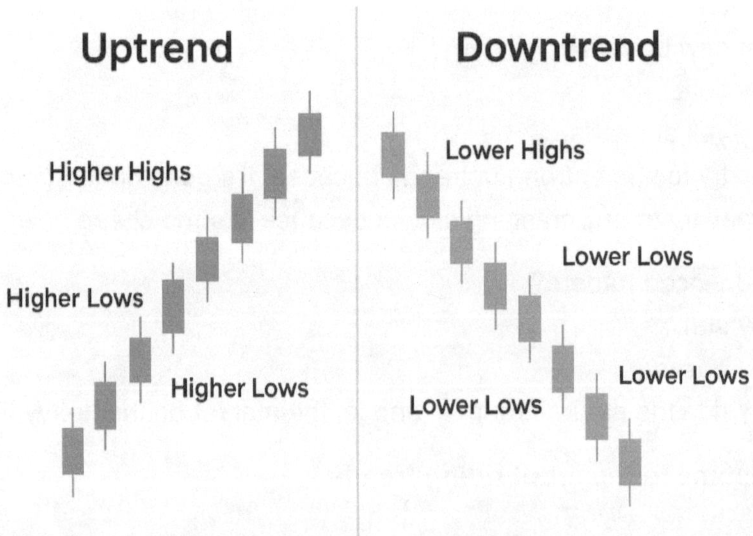

🧠 Why Traders Lose to Trends (Again and Again)

Most traders lose not because they pick bad stocks.
They lose because they fight the obvious.

- They short a rising stock because "it can't go higher."
- They buy a crashing stock because "it's already fallen so much."

But here's the brutal truth:

What is strong, often becomes stronger.
What is weak, often becomes weaker.

Fighting trends is like arguing with gravity.
You can scream all you want — you'll still hit the ground.

✅ Smart traders don't predict trend endings.
✅ Smart traders ride trends until proven otherwise.

No ego.
No "it should have reversed" crying.
Only flow.

📚 The Three Natural Stages of Any Trend

Stage 1: Trend Birth — "Is This Real?"

- Breakout from old ranges.
- Early moves with low trust.
- Everyone doubts it: "Fakeout again?"

This is when snipers quietly observe, prepare — while the crowd mocks.

Stage 2: Trend Expansion — "Everyone Wants In"

- Price gains speed.
- Pullbacks are shallow and get bought quickly.
- News articles start talking about "the unstoppable rally."

This is where real trend riders make serious gains —

while new traders FOMO and jump in at bad entries.

Stage 3: Trend Exhaustion — "Party is Over"

- Volatility rises.
- Reversals become frequent.
- Volume dries up.

But notice:
Sniper traders are exiting positions **before** the ugly reversals — because they ride until the wave weakens, not until it crashes on their heads.

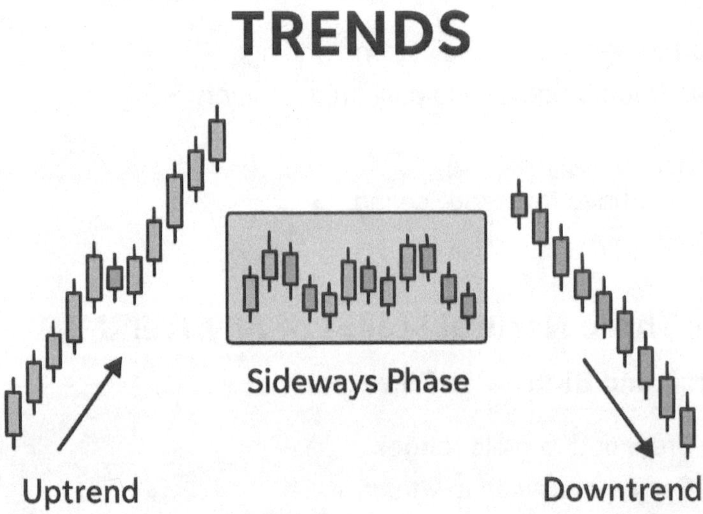

☑ How Professional Traders Ride Trends Smoothly

You don't need 27 indicators.
You don't need astrology predictions.

You need **structure, flow, and discipline**.

Simple tools sniper traders use:

- **20 EMA:** Short-term health check.
- **50 EMA:** Mid-term trend tracker.
- **200 EMA:** Long-term trend spine.

If price stays above 20 EMA and 50 EMA —
you ride it.

If price stays below —
you stay out, or ride shorts if you're aggressive.

If price is chopping sideways —
you grab a coffee, breathe, and remind yourself: "No wave, no surf today."

🛡 Real Battle Story: Tata Motors — Ride or Cry

In early 2025, Tata Motors broke ₹650 resistance.

- Traders who doubted kept shorting every new high.
- They got steamrolled again... and again... and again.

Meanwhile, sniper traders who simply:

- Entered on breakout
- Rode the 20 EMA pullbacks
- Let price breathe
- Exited only when trend weakened

...watched price rally from ₹650 to ₹840 in three months.

✅ No fancy predictions.
✅ No 20 WhatsApp groups shouting "top is in!"
✅ Just riding the wave — calmly, silently, professionally.

Be that trader.

🎯 Action Plan After Chapter 4:

✅ Study 5 strong trends from the last 12 months (Nifty, BankNifty, Tata Motors, Reliance, ICICI Bank).
✅ For each:

- Mark the trend birth, expansion, and exhaustion.
- Mark how price interacted with 20 EMA and 50 EMA.
- Write down what you would have done differently.

✅ Start building your internal "Trend Library."
The more you train your sniper eyes,
the faster you'll spot the early stages of new waves.

🧘 Final Mentor Tip:

In trading, it's not the smart who win.
It's the disciplined who win.

You don't have to predict trends.
You just have to recognize them early, ride them calmly, and exit before the fools realize it's over.

Trade with humility.
Surf the market's energy — not your ego.

Become the silent warrior of trends.

🎯

Chapter 5

Moving Averages — 20 EMA, 50 EMA, 200 EMA Secrets

📝 Introduction:

"Not Magic Lines. Real Dynamic Maps."

When most new traders hear "moving average,"
their eyes glaze over like a Monday morning Zoom call. 😴

Lines on a chart? So what?

But in the hands of a sniper trader,
moving averages become deadly accurate tools —
guiding entries, exits, trend confirmation, and even warning you when the battlefield is changing.

Moving averages are not magic wands.
They are **dynamic maps** —
showing you the path of least resistance.

Learn to read them with intelligence,
and you'll ride trends smoothly while others panic at every candle.

📈 What is a Moving Average?

A **Moving Average** simply smoothens out price action by averaging the past price data over a specific period.

Imagine it like this:

If raw price is a noisy crowd shouting random things —

the moving average is the calm, wise voice summarizing what the crowd *really* feels.

✅ Helps you see the real trend
✅ Reduces emotional noise
✅ Gives clean zones for sniper entries

There are many types, but the two most useful for traders are:

- **Simple Moving Average (SMA)**: Straight average
- **Exponential Moving Average (EMA)**: More weight on recent prices (more responsive, better for traders)

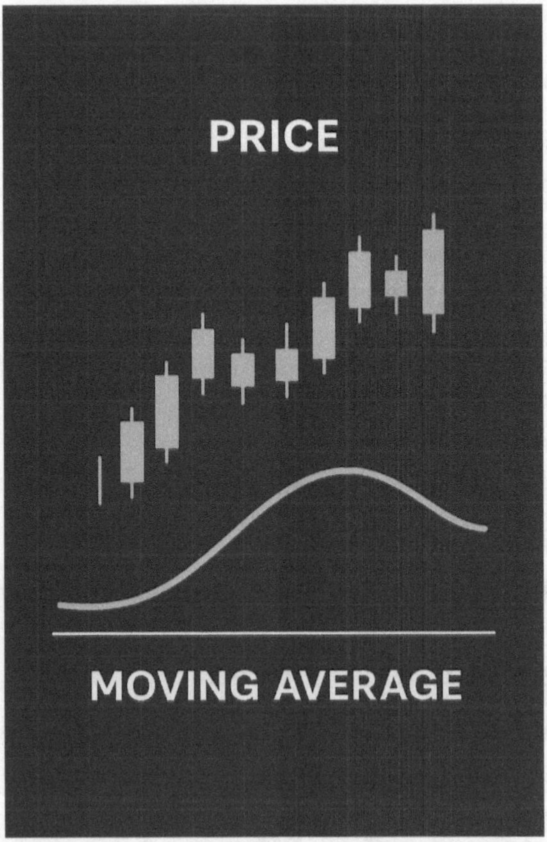

🧐 Why We Focus on 20 EMA, 50 EMA, 200 EMA

You could use 1000 indicators.
But sniper traders stick to a few proven weapons.

20 EMA – The Sniper's Short-Term Lens

- Hugs price tightly.
- Shows short-term trend health.
- Great for fast traders (intraday, swing).

👉 If price is respecting 20 EMA, trend momentum is strong.
👉 If price slices through 20 EMA aggressively, momentum is weakening.

50 EMA – The Midfield General

- More forgiving than 20 EMA.
- Tracks the medium-term flow.

👉 Pullbacks to 50 EMA often give golden sniper entries during healthy trends.

200 EMA – The Battlefield Spine

- Tracks the long-term health of price.
- Used by institutions, funds, algos.
- Often acts like a giant magnet during massive trends.

👉 If price is above 200 EMA, bulls are generally in control.
👉 If below 200 EMA, bears have the edge.

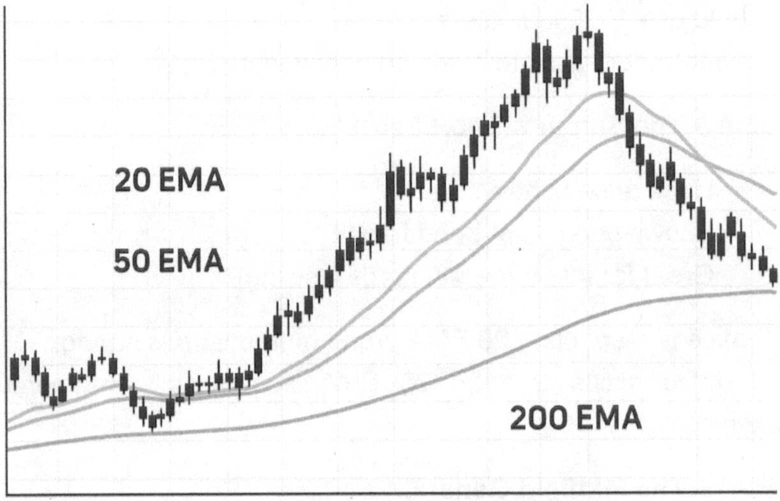

💰 The Real Secret — Dynamic Support and Resistance

Moving averages are **NOT just trend indicators**.
They also act as **dynamic Support and Resistance zones**.

- During strong uptrends, price bounces off 20 EMA or 50 EMA.
- During downtrends, price gets rejected at 20 EMA or 50 EMA.

It's like the market leaves invisible footprints:
"Hey, watch this 20 EMA, it matters."

But remember:

> **The MA is not magic.**
> **It's a reference. Price action + context matter more.**

Snipers always observe **how price behaves at moving averages**, not just blindly react when price touches them.

🗄 Real Quick Example: BankNifty EMA Ride

March 2025:
BankNifty rallies 1800 points over 2 weeks.

- Every pullback kisses the 20 EMA — then rockets.
- Price never even touched the 50 EMA.

Traders who waited for "deep pullbacks" missed the entire trend.
Snipers who respected the 20 EMA flow?
They rode the wave like pros — no panic, no FOMO.

❗ Rookie Mistakes to Avoid with Moving Averages

- ❌ Blindly buying/selling when price hits an MA.
- ❌ Using too many EMAs (clutter = confusion).
- ❌ Ignoring the bigger trend structure.

MAs guide you.
They don't control the market.

Your job is not to worship them —
it's to combine them smartly with price action and market context.

🎯 Action Plan After Chapter 5:

✅ Open charts of Nifty, BankNifty, Reliance, Tata Motors.
✅ Plot 20 EMA, 50 EMA, and 200 EMA.
✅ Study:

- How price reacts at 20 EMA during strong trends
- How deeper pullbacks happen to 50 EMA
- How 200 EMA acts during major crashes/rallies

✅ Screenshot 5 clean examples of price respecting MA zones.
✅ Start building your "Moving Average Pattern Library."

The market repeats its habits for those who have eyes trained to see it.

Final Mentor Tip:

Moving averages are not crystal balls.
They are compasses.

Use them to guide your direction.
Use them to spot when the wind is changing.
But always — always — listen to price itself first.

Trade smart.
Ride trends calmly.
Let the amateurs chase random indicators while you flow like a true market sniper.

🎯

Chapter 6

Breakouts and False Breakouts — Scalp Smart

✍ Introduction:

"Not Every Firework Ends With a Celebration."

Have you ever seen a firecracker that lights up, builds excitement, and then... just fizzles out with a sad puff of smoke? 🎆😑

That's exactly what a false breakout feels like in trading.

You see a candle blast through resistance.
Volume spikes.
Everyone screams "Breakout!"
You enter.
And within minutes... you're trapped. The market reverses. You're holding a loss. 💔

Real breakout trading is about timing.
Real breakout survival is about patience.

This chapter is your guide to tell the difference — and scalp smart.

🧠 What is a Breakout?

A **breakout** is when price escapes a significant level:

- A strong resistance is broken upward (bullish breakout)
- A strong support is broken downward (bearish breakout)

But a true breakout is not just a line getting crossed.

It's **the emotional explosion** of trapped traders being forced to react.

✅ Breakouts happen because buyers overpower sellers — or vice-versa — **not because a line got drawn.**

📖 Mini Story: The Real Breakout Party

Imagine Nifty stuck under 22,450 for 3 days.

Every time it reaches 22,450 — it gets slapped down.
Sellers grow confident.
Buyers hesitate.

Then one day —

- A huge bullish candle bursts above 22,450
- Volume spikes
- Price closes firmly above

You can literally **feel** the emotion:

- Sellers are trapped and forced to cover (adding fuel to fire)
- New buyers jump in, creating momentum

✅ THAT'S a true breakout.

Clean Breakout

🛡 How to Confirm a Real Breakout (Sniper Checklist)

Before you trust any breakout, check:

1. **Volume Spike:**

   Real breakouts have heavy volume. Fakeouts are quiet.

2. **Candle Body Close:**

   Breakout candles should have large, healthy bodies — not tiny wicks or indecision candles.

3. **Retest Behavior (Optional but Powerful):**

   If price retests the broken level and holds — sniper-grade confirmation.

4. **Market Context:**

   Is this breakout in the direction of higher timeframe trend?
   (Example: 5-min breakout aligning with 1-hour uptrend = 🔥)

🛑 What is a False Breakout (Trap)?

A **false breakout** is the ultimate trap for impatient traders.

The market **pretends** to break out — just enough to lure buyers/ sellers —

then **slams back inside the range**, stopping out everyone who chased emotionally.

It's not a mistake.
It's **planned battlefield psychology**.

- Big players trigger stop-hunts.
- Trapped amateurs panic-sell or panic-cover.
- Smart money scoops up positions calmly.

📖 Mini Story: The Trap at 23,000

BankNifty flirts with 23,000.

You see a quick breakout —
but the candle closes with a massive upper wick.
Volume? Barely higher.

Minutes later — BankNifty reverses, crashes 300 points.

Amateurs cry:

> "Market is manipulated!"

Snipers smile:

> "It was obvious."

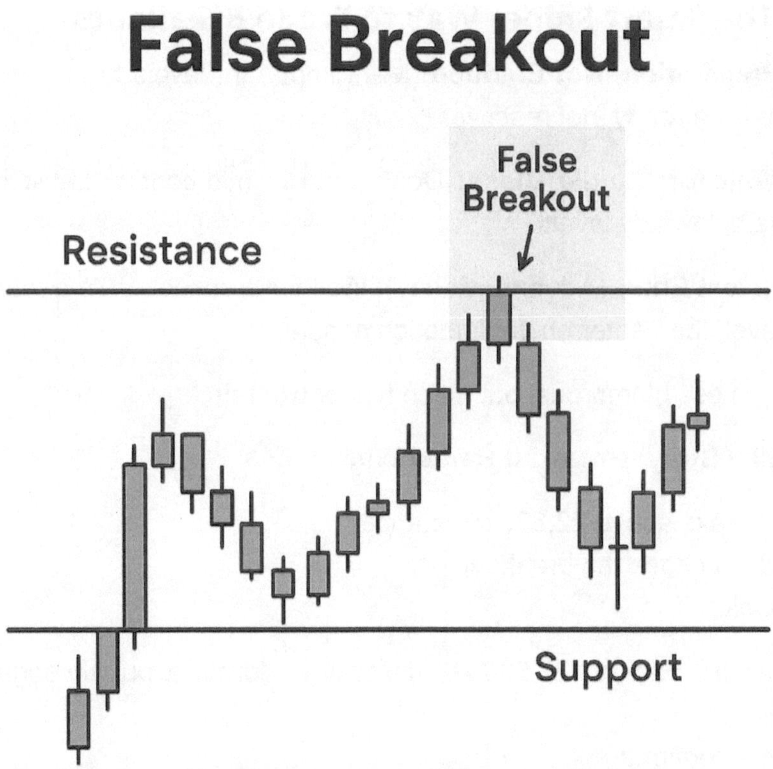

🧠 How to Spot a Potential False Breakout

✅ Breakout Candle is Weak:
Small body, big wicks = No conviction.

✅ Volume is Missing:
Low volume breakout = Fake move.

✅ Immediate Rejection:
If next candle slams back into the range — trap confirmed.

✅ Divergence with Momentum Indicators:
Example: Price makes new high but RSI/MACD show lower highs.

If any two signs align — STAY OUT.
No trade is better than a bad trade.

🎯 The Smart Sniper Way to Trade Breakouts

✅ **Preparation, Not Emotion:** Mark important levels before market open — be ready, not reactive.

✅ **Wait for Candle Close:** Don't jump in mid-candle. Let it close above/below key levels.

✅ **Retest Entry (Advanced Play):** Wait for breakout, then a retest of the level, then enter on confirmation candle.

Less glamorous, but much higher win rate.

📖 Mini Story: Breakout Retest Win

Nifty breaks above 22,800 resistance.
You don't chase the breakout.
You wait.

Price pulls back to 22,800 — kisses it — forms a bullish engulfing candle.
Volume confirms.

You enter.

Low risk. High confidence.

Two hours later, you're deep in profit — while impulsive traders are still licking their wounds.

BREAKOUT AND RETEST EXAMPLE

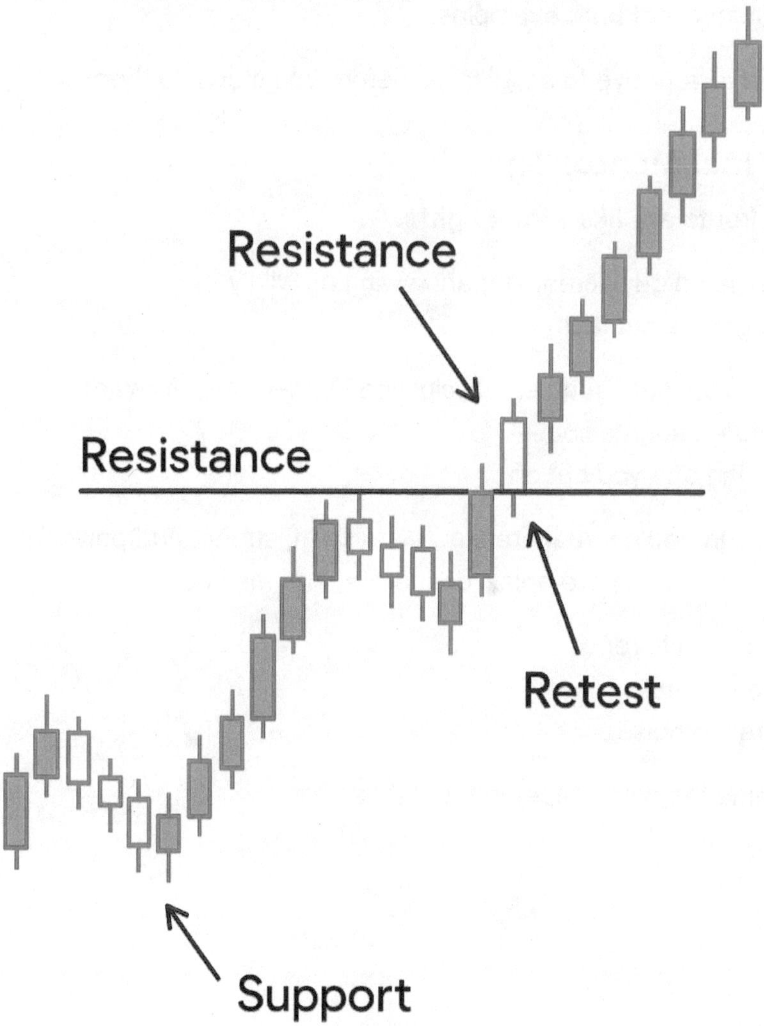

🎯 Action Plan After Chapter 6:

✅ Study 10 recent breakouts and false breakouts:

- 5 true breakouts (high volume, strong close, retest)
- 5 false breakouts (weak candles, no volume, immediate reversals)

✅ Screenshot both examples.

✅ Train your eye to smell traps before you step into them.

🧘 Final Mentor Tip:

Breakouts are like street fights.

If you see a guy screaming and swinging wildly —
he might tire out fast.

But if you see a quiet, disciplined fighter step forward with calm, measured aggression —
that's the one you bet on.

> In trading, real breakouts are calm, strong, and powerful.
> Fakeouts are noisy, desperate, and messy.

Learn the difference.
Trade the real.
Ignore the noise.

Become the calm sniper in the chaos.

Chapter 7

Volume Analysis — The Power Behind Price

✍ Introduction:

"Price moves. But volume reveals why."

Imagine you're in a crowded market.
One shop suddenly drops its prices.
People rush in — grabbing everything.
You don't just see the price change.
You feel the **intensity**, the **urgency**, the **volume of action** behind it.

That's exactly what **volume** is in trading.
It tells you if a price move is just a weak whisper…
or a war cry from smart money.

Most traders stare at candles.
But the real edge comes when you start listening to **how loud those candles actually are.**
Because price can lie. But volume?
Volume exposes the truth.

🧠 Why Volume Matters More Than You Think

Price tells you what is happening.
But volume tells you **who's behind it** — and how committed they are.

- Is this breakout real?
- Is this pullback a trap?
- Is this range about to explode?

  You won't know unless you check:

  "How loud is the market right now?"

Volume is like the *heartbeat of the move*.
If it's silent, the move won't last.
If it's roaring, it's likely legit.

📖 Story: The Fake Breakout That Fooled Everyone (Except the Snipers)

Tata Motors is at ₹950 — a known resistance.
You see a breakout candle.
Looks bullish. Strong close.

But something feels... off.

You check volume:
✅ It's actually *lower* than the last 3 candles.

No big players stepped in.

Just noise.

You don't enter.

30 minutes later, the price crashes back below ₹950, taking out everyone who blindly bought the breakout.

You?
Sitting relaxed.
Watching the drama unfold.
Not a scratch on you.

That's the power of volume.

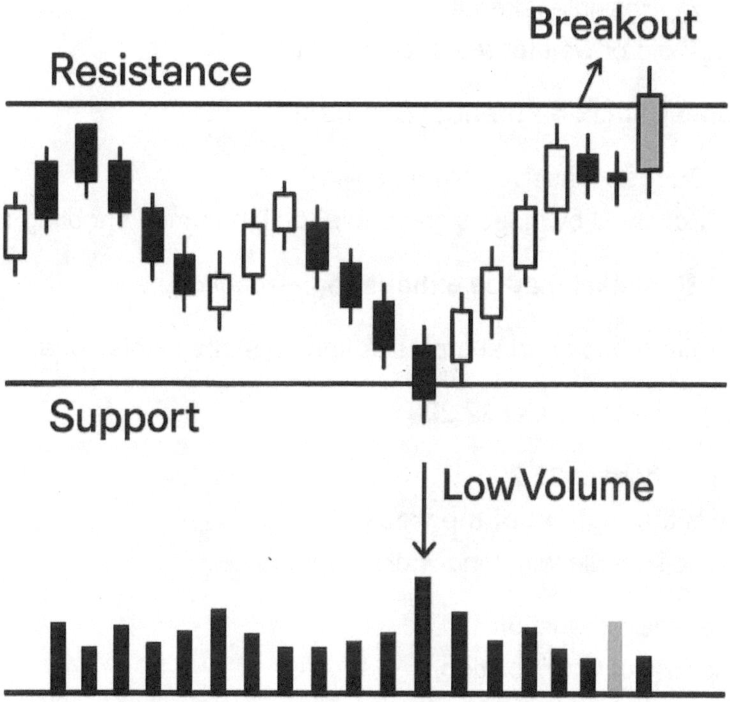

🔍 The 3 Volume Scenarios That Matter Most

Let's simplify.
You don't need 50 rules — just these **3 golden volume reads**:

1. Volume Surge on Breakout = Real Move

- If price breaks a key level
- And volume spikes higher than last 10–15 candles

  ✅ You're seeing **smart money entering**
  This is the green zone.

2. Breakout Without Volume = Trap Alert

- If price breaks resistance
- But volume is weak or average

⚠ Possible fakeout
Avoid or wait for retest confirmation.

3. Volume Climax = Potential Reversal

- Sudden massive volume spike
- Followed by indecision candle (doji, hammer, shooting star)

🛑 Market may be **exhausting** — caution here.

Smart traders book partial profits or tighten stops in this zone.

📖 Story: The Climax at 22,200

Nifty rallies hard to 22,200
Volume is the **highest of the week**
Then: A doji candle with long wicks appears

You smell the exhaustion.
You exit 75% of your position.
Next day — Nifty drops 120 points.

Others are shocked.
You sleep well.

Breakout with Strong Volume

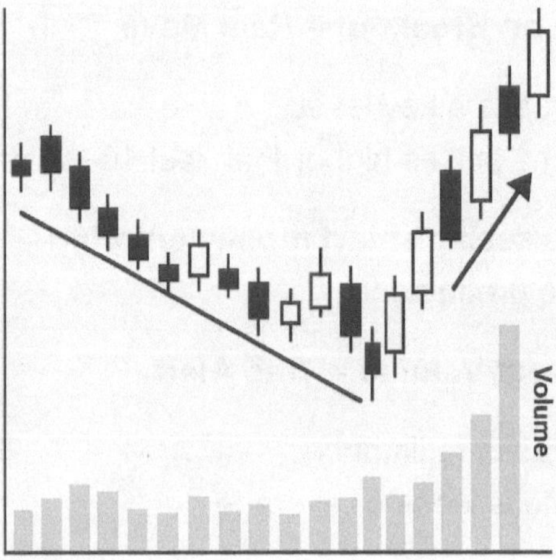

🧠 Volume by Itself is Powerful — But Combine it for Mastery

Volume + Candlestick = Emotional pulse
Volume + Support/Resistance = Battle intensity
Volume + RSI/MACD = Setup confirmation

It's not about volume spikes alone.
It's about seeing **how volume supports or betrays** price.

Always ask:

> "If I were a big player… would I be entering here with size?"
> If volume says "yes" — go.
> If not? Walk away.

📖 Story: The Hidden Buyer at ₹620

You're watching HDFC Bank grind down slowly to ₹620
Price looks weak
But you notice something strange...

Each red candle has **shrinking volume**
Then — one small green candle with **huge volume spike**

Someone is loading up quietly.

Next session: Boom. ₹620 to ₹635 in 3 candles.

Everyone asks "What happened?"

You already knew:
The buyer showed their hand… **through volume**.

VOLUME DIVERGENCE

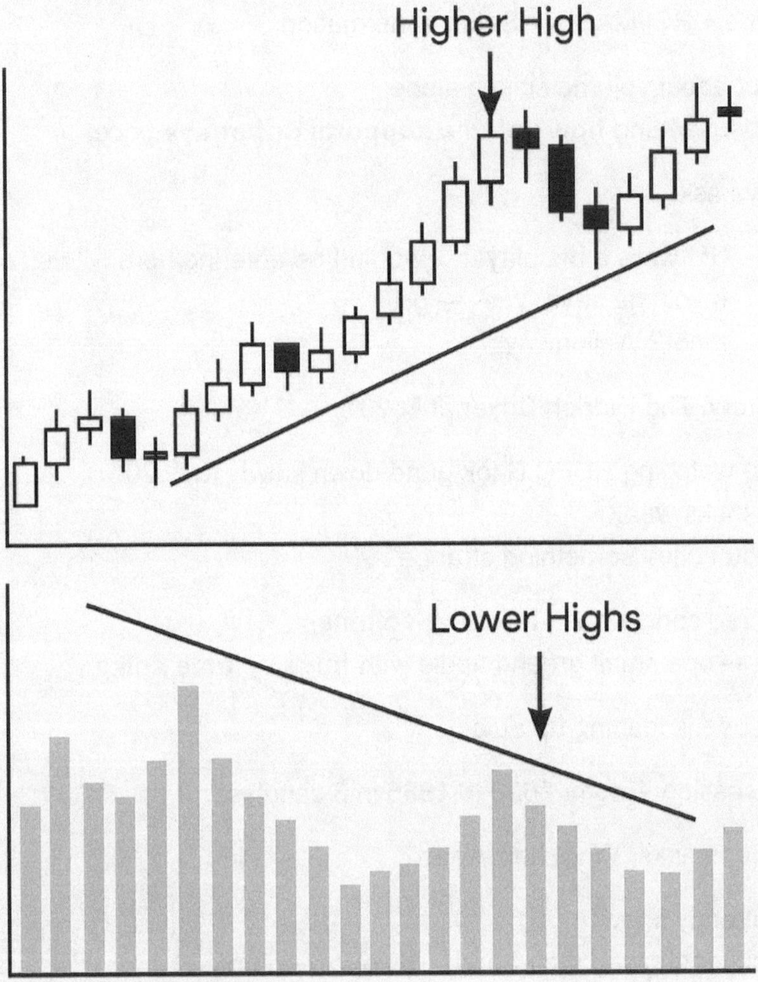

🎯 Action Plan After Chapter 7:

- ✅ Study 5 clean breakouts
- ✅ Study 5 fake breakouts
- ✅ Compare volume strength in each

☑ Mark 3 spots where:

- Price reversed after volume climax
- Price exploded after silent volume loading

☑ Start your **Volume Pattern Journal** — because once your eye learns volume behavior,
you'll never fall for surface-level moves again.

🧘 Final Mentor Tip:

Candles tell the story.
Volume reveals the truth.

You can lie with price.
But you can't lie with commitment.

Smart traders follow the real flow —
the big buyers, the big sellers, the crowd shifts.

Volume shows them.
If you learn to listen…
you won't just trade charts anymore —
you'll trade the **heartbeat of the market.**

🧠

Chapter 8

RSI, MACD, and Momentum — Confirmations That Actually Work

✍ Introduction:

"Indicators don't lead the market — they confirm it."

Most traders slap on RSI and MACD like toppings on a pizza.
No context. No structure. Just vibes. 🍕

But the truth is — indicators like **RSI, MACD, and other momentum tools** are not meant to predict moves.
They're meant to **confirm your edge**.

You don't use them to ask,

> "Should I buy now?"

You use them to ask,

> "Does this setup feel real? Or is the market playing games with me?"

In this chapter, you'll learn how to use RSI, MACD, and momentum like a **silent advisor** — not a noisy DJ.

🔍 Understanding Momentum

Momentum is simple:
It tells you **how fast and strong** a move is happening.

Just like a car:

- Speeding up = growing trend
- Slowing down = potential reversal
- Still moving, but weaker? = caution zone

Momentum indicators show you **the emotional intensity** behind price —
whether the move is powered by conviction…
or running out of fuel.

📈 RSI — The Emotional Thermometer

RSI (Relative Strength Index) measures the speed of recent price movements on a 0–100 scale.

- **Above 70** = Traditionally "overbought"
- **Below 30** = Traditionally "oversold"

But here's the truth:

> **Strong trends stay overbought or oversold longer than you think.**

Amateur traders panic when RSI touches 70 — they short it.
Only to watch the price rip even higher. 💀

✅ Pro traders use RSI to:

- Confirm breakout strength
- Spot divergence (when price moves opposite to RSI)
- Read *when* a market is stretched vs. when it's truly exhausted

📖 Story: The Overbought Trap

BankNifty rallies and RSI hits 75.
Twitter floods with "OVERBOUGHT!!!"

But you zoom out.
Price is in a strong uptrend, riding the 20 EMA.
You know RSI is **confirming strength** — not warning of collapse.

So while others short early,
you ride the trend clean to the next leg.

RSI Staying Overbought in Strong Uptrend

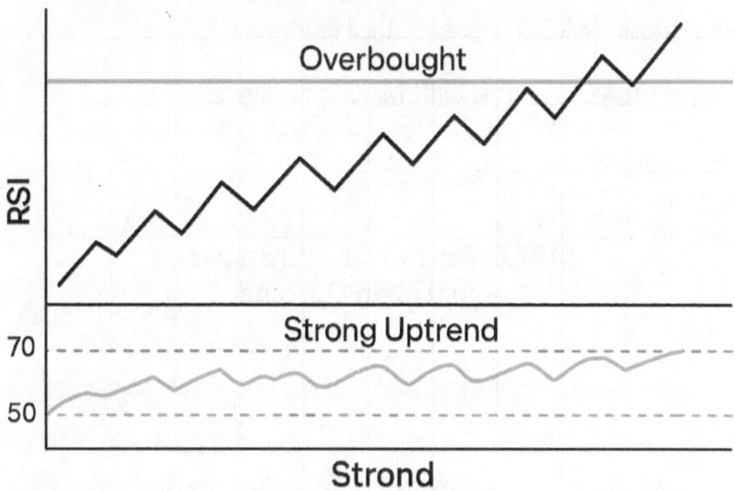

📈 MACD — The Trend Shifter

MACD (Moving Average Convergence Divergence) shows:

- Trend direction
- Trend strength
- Momentum shifts before price turns

MACD works on two EMAs (12 & 26), plus a signal line.

✅ When MACD Line crosses above the Signal Line = **Bullish**
✅ When MACD Line crosses below = **Bearish**
✅ When the Histogram shrinks = **Momentum fading**
✅ When it expands = **Strength building**

But here's the sniper truth:

> **MACD rarely gives early signals.**
> **It gives strong confirmation when paired with price action.**

📖 Story: The Quiet MACD Flip

You're watching Reliance consolidate near ₹2,900
MACD was negative — but now slowly curling upward
Price breaks out. MACD crosses up. Histogram grows.

You take the breakout trade with MACD confirmation.

It's not a prediction.
It's conviction.

MACD Fails to Give Crossover Signal in an Uptrend

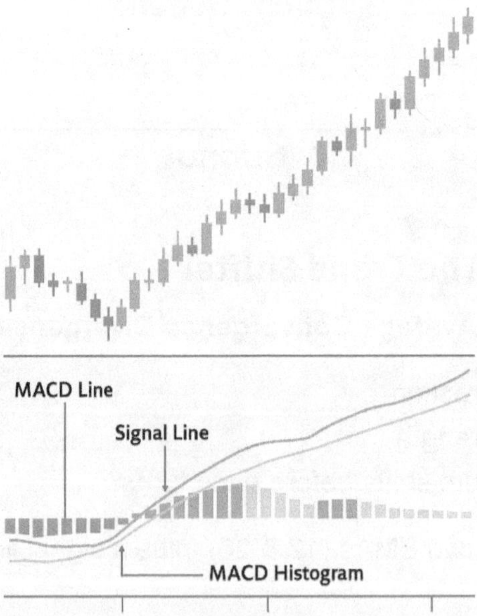

🧠 How to Combine RSI + MACD for Killer Confirmation

✅ If RSI is above 50 and MACD gives a bullish crossover:

Price has strength + momentum = 🔥 setup

✅ If RSI is falling while MACD gives a fake crossover:

Likely trap. Wait.

✅ If both indicators show divergence vs. price:

Reversal might be near. Tighten stops.

You don't need to be an expert on indicator math.

You just need to see when **indicators agree with price** — and when they're screaming **"Wait!"**

📉 Momentum Divergence — The Hidden Warning

Divergence happens when **price makes new highs/lows** but **momentum does not.**

This is often a sniper clue:

- Trend is tiring
- Market is stretched
- Reversal likely near

Look for:

- RSI divergence
- MACD divergence
- Volume drop + divergence = major reversal potential

🕮 Story: The Final Push That Failed

Tata Motors hits a new high — ₹1,020
But RSI? Flat.
MACD? Shrinking histogram.

You stay out.

Next day — price crashes 3%.
Everyone says: "But the breakout looked so strong!"

You say: "Not to RSI. Not to MACD."

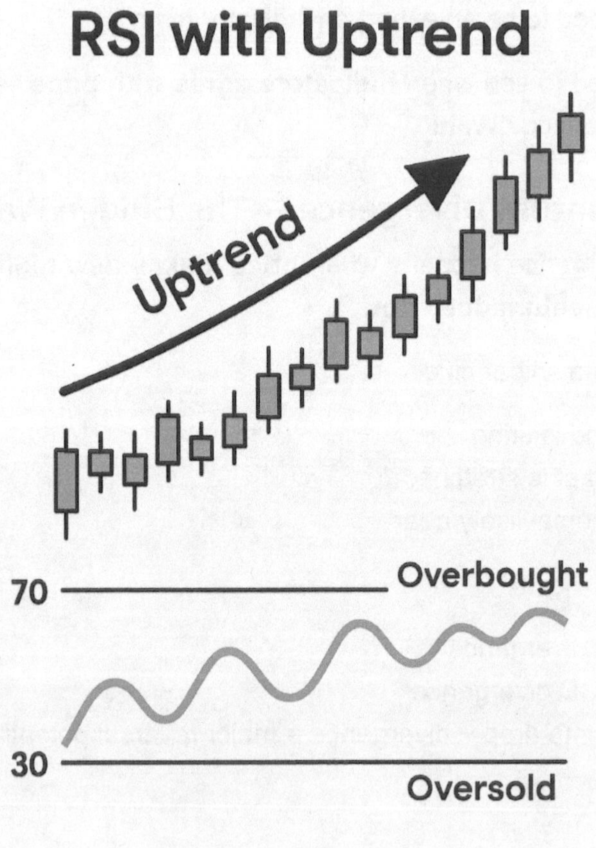

Bullish candistick

🎯 Action Plan After Chapter 8:

✅ Review 10 breakout trades from the last month.
✅ Check if RSI/MACD agreed or disagreed with price.
✅ Journal which trades succeeded with confirmation — and which ones failed without it.

✅ Start building your "Momentum Confidence Tracker" —
A simple sheet that tells you:

> "When price + RSI + MACD aligned → How often did the trade win?"

You'll be shocked at how clear your setups become.

🧘 Final Mentor Tip:

Indicators are not magic.
They are just mirrors.

They reflect what price is already trying to say —
if you know how to listen.

Trade like a detective.
Let price action tell you the story.
Let RSI and MACD help you confirm if it's real.

Don't follow the indicators.
Use them to support your truth.

That's how sniper traders move:
Silent. Prepared. Confirmed.

🧩

Chapter 9

Multi-Timeframe Analysis — Seeing the Full Picture

🖊 Introduction:

"Zoom out. Or get zoomed out of the market."

Ever tried to read a map by staring at a single building?
You won't know if it's on a highway or a dead-end street.
Same with trading.

A 5-minute chart might show a breakout —
But the 1-hour chart? It's inside a bigger resistance.
Now you're trapped... not because you were wrong,
but because you were **too zoomed in**.

This chapter is about learning to zoom out, align your view, and make decisions like a market sniper —
from the top down.

🔍 What is Multi-Timeframe Analysis (MTA)?

It's the art of using **multiple timeframes** to understand:

- The broader market context
- The medium-term setup
- The precise entry zone

Think of it like using:

- **1-Hour Chart** → Satellite View
- **15-Minute Chart** → Drone View
- **5-Minute Chart** → Sniper Scope

When all 3 tell the same story,
you get confidence like a soldier with air support.

📖 Story: The Fakeout That Fooled the Zoomed-In Trader

It's Wednesday.
BankNifty's 5-min chart breaks above 47,000.
You jump in — excited. Clean candle. Looks bullish.

Then BOOM.
10 minutes later it crashes 120 points. SL hit. You're stunned.

You switch to 1-hour chart…
And it shows price **rejecting a major resistance zone**.
There was never any strength — just a trap.

You weren't wrong.
You were just looking **too close, too soon.**

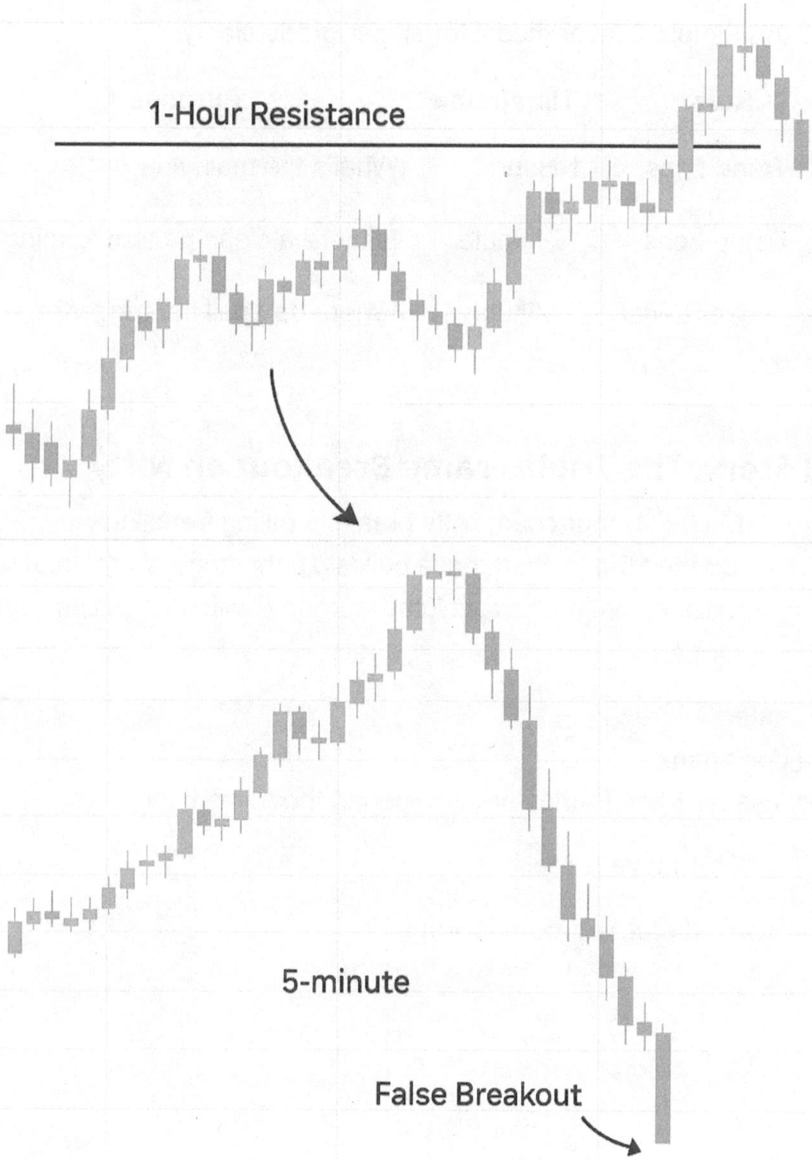
1-Hour Resistance
5-minute
False Breakout

🧭 The 3-Frame Setup: Your Trading Lens

Use this simple 3-layer model for sniper-grade clarity:

Role	Timeframe	Purpose
🧭 Trend Lens	1-Hour	What's the main flow?
🔍 Setup Lens	15-Minute	Is there a clean pattern forming?
🎯 Trigger Lens	5-Minute	Where do I pull the trigger?

📖 Story: The Triple Frame Breakout on Nifty

- On the 1-hour chart, Nifty breaks a falling trendline
- On the 15-min chart, price builds a tight range at breakout level
- On the 5-min chart, volume surges, bullish engulfing candle forms

You enter.
You don't panic.
Because all 3 timeframes are whispering the same thing:

> "This move is real."

That's called **stacked conviction.**

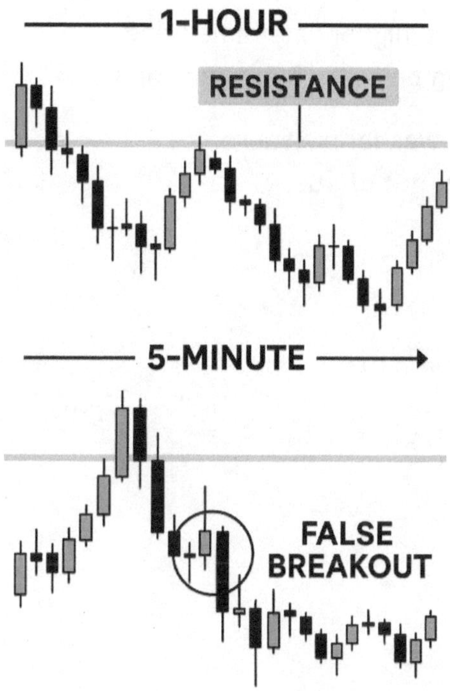

⬣ What to Do When Timeframes Disagree?

- 1-Hour = Uptrend
- 15-Min = Sideways
- 5-Min = Looks bearish

☞ What do you do?

You don't trade.

Mismatched timeframes = confusion
Confusion = hesitation
Hesitation = SL hits

The market isn't ready.
So neither are you.

Sniper traders only act when the battlefield is clear.

🧘 Secret Benefit: MTA = Emotional Control

When you know the higher timeframe trend...
You stop panicking on every 5-min red candle.

You can **breathe**, wait for pullbacks,
and act with **calm, not chaos.**

Chapter 10

VWAP and EMAs for Scalping — Intraday Sniper Tools

✍ Introduction:

"If you blink, you miss the shot. Welcome to scalping."

Scalping isn't for everyone.
It's fast. It's brutal. It tests your nerves.
But in the hands of a **calm, system-driven trader**,
scalping can be a silent, consistent income machine.

The trick?
You don't chase.
You don't guess.
You just learn to read **VWAP and EMAs** —
and let them guide you like a laser scope.

This chapter will teach you how real scalpers use VWAP and EMAs — **not like decoration on the chart**, but like combat-grade targeting systems.

🧠 First — What is Scalping?

Scalping means:

- Getting in fast
- Getting out faster

- Taking small profits, repeatedly
- Protecting capital like your life depends on it

It's not about predicting big trends.
It's about catching the **micro-moves within the bigger structure.**

And for that, your best allies are:

- **VWAP** = The battlefield control line
- **EMAs (20, 50)** = Your directional pulse

☑ VWAP — Volume Weighted Average Price

Think of VWAP as the **fair price zone** of the day.

- Price above VWAP? Buyers dominate
- Price below VWAP? Sellers dominate
- Price hovering around VWAP? No clear control — stay cautious

Institutions use VWAP to benchmark their entries.
Scalpers use VWAP to decide whether to strike **with** or **against** momentum.

📖 Story: The VWAP Battle in Nifty

It's 10:15 AM.
Nifty is chopping around.
Price breaks above VWAP. Volume ticks up.

You don't rush in.
You wait for one clean 5-minute bullish candle to hold **above VWAP**.

✅ You enter.
✅ SL just below VWAP.
✅ Target = 0.5% move or fixed RR.

You're out in 7 minutes.
Clean win. No stress.
Why? Because VWAP confirmed who had control.

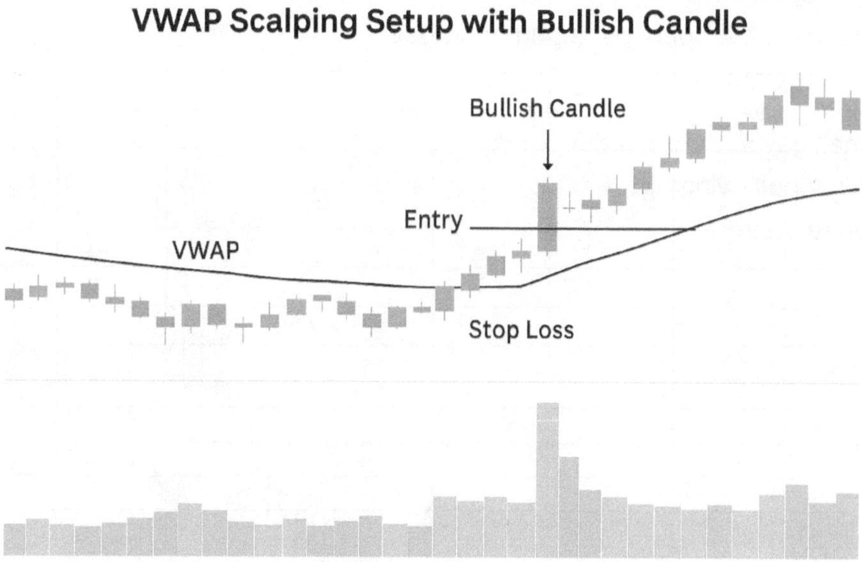

EMAs (20, 50) — The Scalper's Flow Meter

20 EMA = Short-term price momentum
50 EMA = Micro trend confirmation

When:

- 20 EMA is above 50 EMA = Bull bias
- Price bouncing off 20 EMA = Active buyers
- Price respecting both = Steady trending opportunity

Scalpers use these EMAs not as magical signals,
but as a **map of trend strength and flow.**

Story: The 20 EMA Ride on BankNifty

BankNifty opens strong.
Price breaks above VWAP and hugs the 20 EMA.
Every dip = a small green candle bouncing off the 20 EMA.

You don't guess.
You scalp the bounces, again and again —
like a rhythm.

Small gains. Zero FOMO.
You're not swinging.
You're slicing.

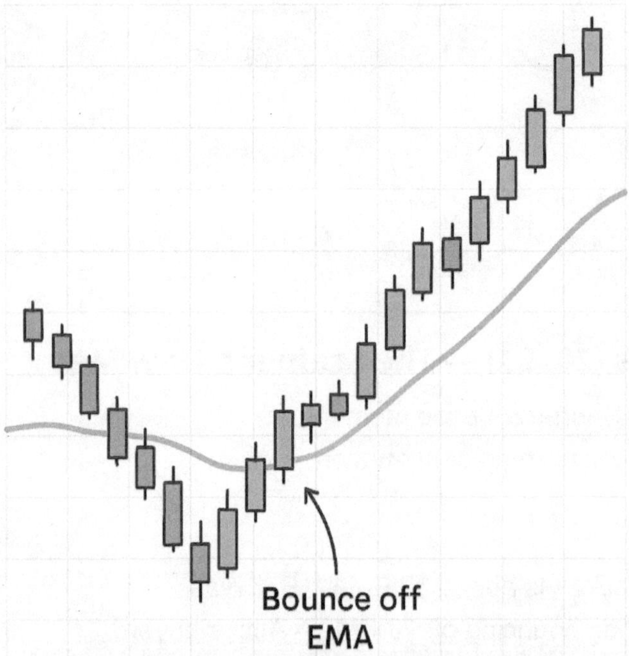

🔥 VWAP + EMA Combo = Deadly Scalping Precision

The magic happens when **VWAP and EMAs align**.

- Price above VWAP
- 20 EMA above 50 EMA
- Price bouncing off 20 EMA

✅ Enter on bullish candle
✅ SL = below VWAP
✅ TP = pre-decided 1:1 or 1.5:1

You're not reacting.
You're **executing a system**.

🕮 Quick Snap: The VWAP+EMA Snapback

Price dips toward VWAP.
20 EMA still sloping up.
A hammer candle forms on 5-min.

Volume supports.
You enter.

Snap move up. Exit in 5 mins.
Other traders? Still confused.

You? Already booked. Done for the day.

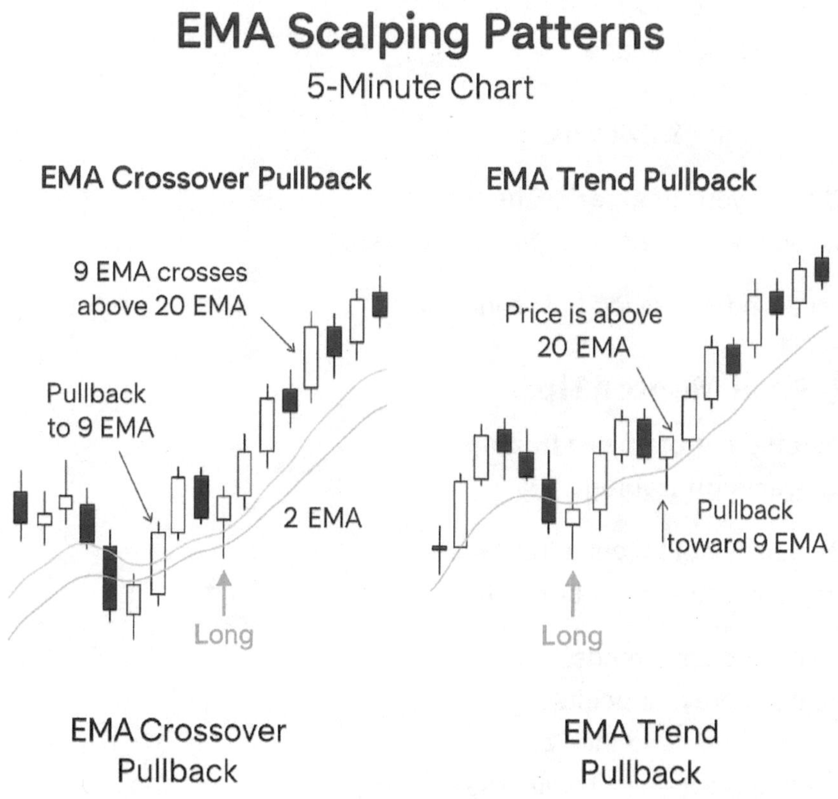

🧠 Key Rules for Scalpers:

☑ Never scalp in low volume ranges
☑ Use only 1 or 2 setups you trust
☑ VWAP is your battlefield line — don't fight against it
☑ Let EMAs show direction, don't blindly enter on crossovers
☑ Small SLs. Fast exits. Zero emotion.

Scalping rewards discipline — not aggression.

🎯 Action Plan After Chapter 10:

☑ Open Nifty, BankNifty intraday charts
☑ Mark 3 clean VWAP scalps and 3 EMA scalps
☑ Note:

- Time
- Candle shape
- Volume
- Entry & Exit logic

☑ Build your **Scalper's Cheat Sheet** —
with setups, visuals, and post-trade lessons

In scalping, repetition builds intuition.

🧘 Final Mentor Tip:

Scalping is not speed trading.
It's precision trading.

The goal is not to feel adrenaline.
The goal is to **stay in control**.

You don't chase trends.
You don't pray for points.
You show up, read the field,
take your shot — and walk away.

VWAP is your shield.
EMAs are your radar.
Discipline is your sword.
Trade fast. Exit faster.
Scalp like a pro. 💥

Chapter 11

Fibonacci Levels — Finding Hidden Supports

✍ Introduction:

"The Market Breathes in Numbers — Learn to Read Its Rhythm."

Have you ever noticed how some pullbacks magically reverse at specific spots?
Like the market hit a pause, took a breath, and moved again?

That's **Fibonacci** in action.

It's not magic. It's not astrology.
It's **probability + structure**.
Fibonacci levels help you identify zones where **price is likely to react** — not because someone predicted it,
but because **millions of traders respect those zones.**

In this chapter, you'll learn how to use Fib levels the right way — like sniper retracement zones, not fantasy lines.

🔍 What is Fibonacci in Trading?

Fibonacci comes from a sequence found in nature (1, 1, 2, 3, 5, 8...)
In trading, we don't care about rabbits or spirals.
We care about the **retracement ratios** derived from this sequence.

Most important levels:

- **0.236** – Shallow pullback
- **0.382** – Initial bounce zone
- **0.5** – Midpoint (not Fibonacci but widely respected)
- **0.618** – The Golden Level
- **0.786** – Deep retrace, last chance before reversal

These levels act like **magnetic zones** —
not guaranteed reversals, but **natural resting points** in price movements.

📖 Story: The Nifty Pullback That Respected Fib to the T

Nifty rallied from 22,000 to 22,800 in 4 days.
Then it started pulling back.

You plot the Fibonacci from swing low (22,000) to swing high (22,800).
Price dips to the **0.382 level (22,500)** — and pauses.
Next day?
Price bounces hard and continues upward.

No news. No special indicator.
Just structure.

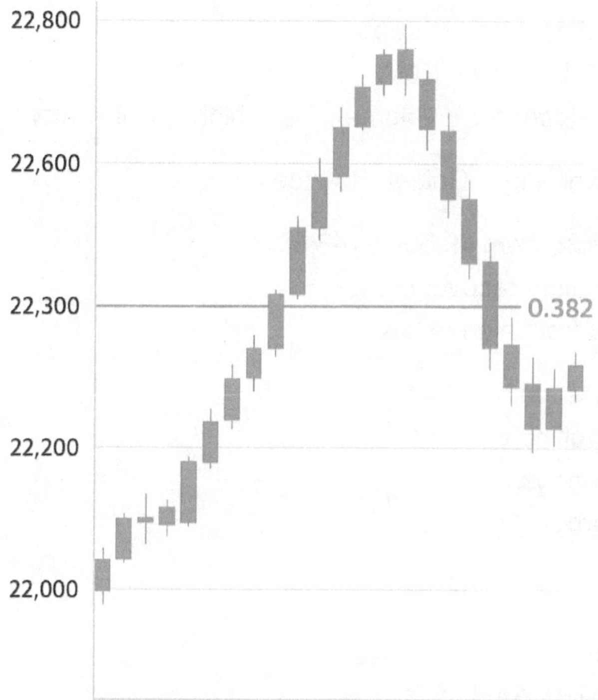

Nifty Pullback to ~0.382 Fibonacci Level

🛠 How to Use Fibonacci (Sniper Style)

1. **Find the Swing**
   - In an uptrend: Drag from low to high
   - In a downtrend: Drag from high to low
2. **Look for Price Reaction Zones**
   - Is price slowing down near 0.382 or 0.618?
   - Candlestick reversal patterns here = potential sniper entry

3. **Combine with Other Tools**
    - Fibonacci + Support Zone
    - Fibonacci + EMA
    - Fibonacci + Volume drop = high-quality entry zone

📖 Story: BankNifty's Golden Bounce

BankNifty drops from 49,500 to 48,000.
Next day — slight recovery.
You drag Fib from high to low.

At **0.618**, price stalls.
A bullish engulfing candle forms.
Volume increases.
20 EMA nearby.

You enter.

Next 90 minutes?
BankNifty rallies 200 points.

You didn't guess.
You read structure + Fib + confirmation = sniper setup.

GBP/INR Pullback to 0.618 Fibonacci Level

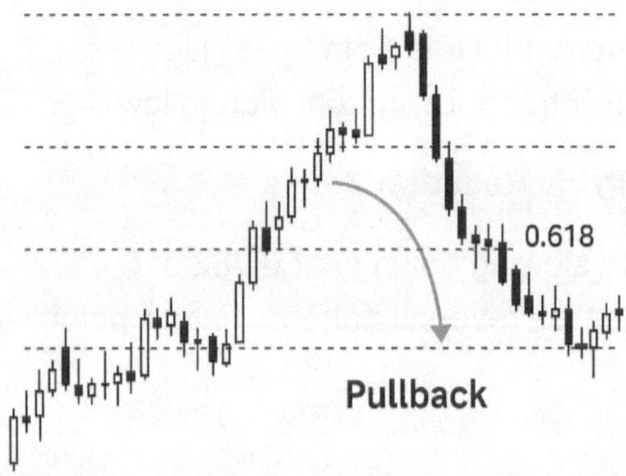

🔥 Pro-Level Trick — Fibonacci Confluence Zones

Sometimes two different swings (short-term and long-term) show overlapping Fib levels.
This is called **confluence** — and it's powerful.

📖 Example:

- Daily swing 0.382 = ₹1,025
- Intraday swing 0.618 = ₹1,026

If price reaches ₹1,025–₹1,026 and forms a reversal candle…
You know **smart money is watching that zone**.
This becomes a **high-conviction entry area**.

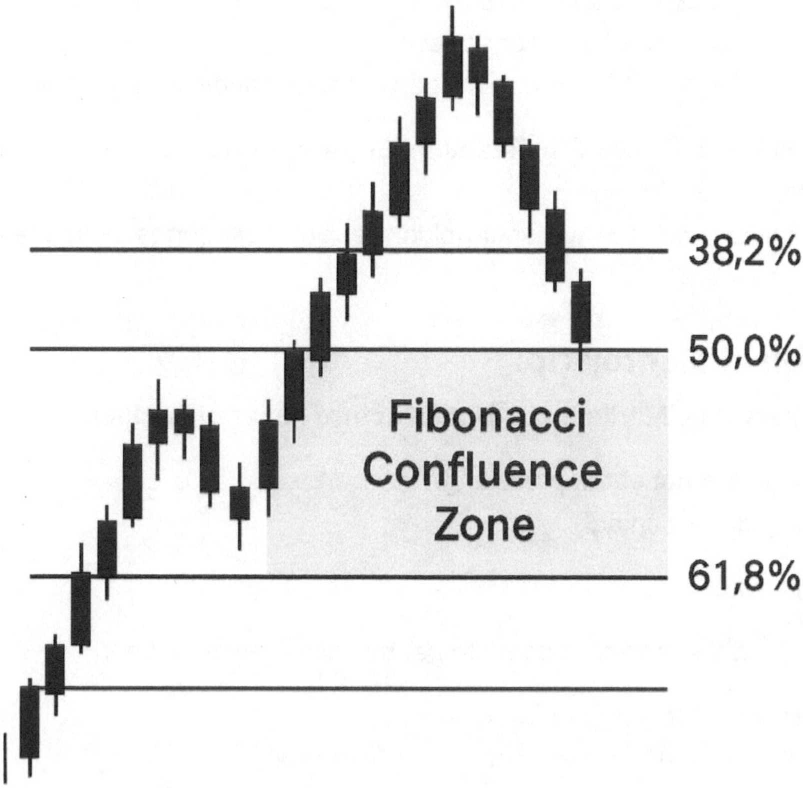

⚠ Mistakes to Avoid:

❌ Drawing Fib randomly on every move
❌ Using Fib without understanding structure
❌ Entering blindly just because price touched a level

Fibonacci is not a trigger. It's a zone of interest.

You still need confirmation from candles, EMAs, or volume.

🎯 Action Plan After Chapter 11:

✅ Pick 3 trending stocks
✅ Use Fib tool on the last impulse move
✅ Mark:

- 0.382, 0.5, and 0.618 levels
- Note price behavior at each
- Capture if there was a clean reversal candle at any zone

✅ Build your own **Fib Reaction Library** — real screenshots, not theory
Over time, your eye will spot golden retracement zones without even drawing them.

🧘 Final Mentor Tip:

Markets rise. Markets fall. But structure never disappears.

Fibonacci is not about predicting.
It's about positioning.

It tells you:

> "If the market is going to pause... it's likely to happen here."

When you stop trying to be right,
and start waiting for **structure + confirmation**,
you become the sniper —
not the prey.

Chapter 12

Psychology of Price Action — Reading the Mind of Market

✍ Introduction:

"The chart isn't just a graph.
It's the collective emotion of millions of traders... including you."

Most traders think price action is about lines, candles, and breakouts.
But price action is really just **emotion, plotted on a chart**.

Fear, greed, FOMO, doubt, overconfidence, hesitation —
they all show up in the **shape** of candles, the **speed** of moves, the **volume** of reactions.

When you begin to **read the psychology behind price**,
you stop reacting to noise —
and start moving with intent.

This chapter teaches you how to **decode emotion** from the chart itself.

🧠 What Is Market Psychology?

Imagine every trader connected to one giant brain.
Some are scared. Some are hopeful. Some are trapped. Some are greedy.
The result of all those emotions?

That's the candle.

So:

- A long wick = rejection
- A sudden spike = panic or aggression
- A tight range = hesitation or balance
- A volume breakout = emotional release

Candlesticks are not just patterns.
They are emotional footprints.

📖 Story: The Trap at 22,000

It's a Monday.
Nifty opens strong. It rockets to 22,000 — breaks above for 5 minutes.

Everyone screams "Breakout!"
You wait.

The breakout candle closes with a long upper wick.
Next candle is red.
Volume spikes.

You smell fear.
You don't chase. You short.

Minutes later — price dumps 150 points.

You didn't trade a pattern.
You traded **emotion under pressure**.

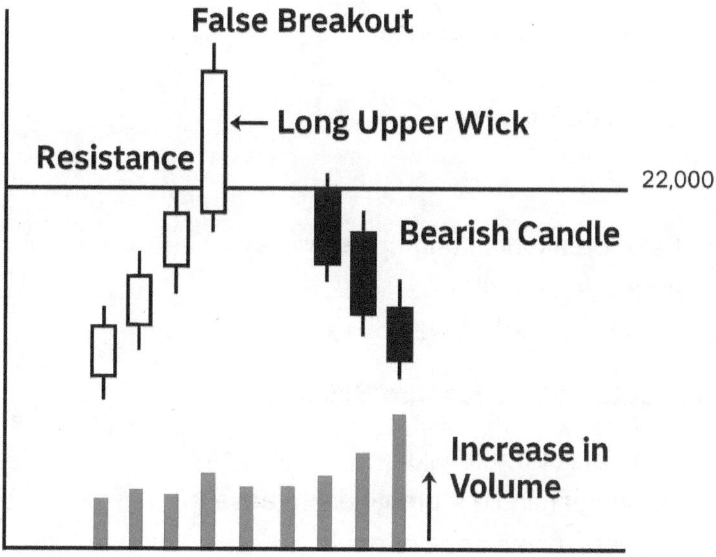

🔍 3 Emotional Zones on Every Chart

Whether it's Nifty, BankNifty, Tata Motors or Apple stock — these **3 zones always reveal psychological warfare**:

1. Support Zones = Hope vs Panic

- Price drops near support
- Buyers hope for bounce
- Sellers watch for breakdown

Look for:

- Wicky candles = buyers trying to defend
- Weak green candles = lack of conviction
- Volume drop = fear is fading

2. Resistance Zones = Greed vs Caution

- Price rises to resistance
- Bulls want breakout
- Bears look to attack

Look for:

- Fake breakouts (long upper wicks)
- Indecision candles
- Volume spike followed by rejection

3. Breakout Zones = Pressure Release

- Long buildup = tension
- Breakout candle = emotional release
- Retest = confidence or doubt

Smart traders don't just chase breakouts.
They ask:

> "Was this breakout based on fear, trap, or true momentum?"

📖 Story: The Retest That Exposed Weak Buyers

Reliance breaks out above ₹2,850
Next candle — weak follow-through
Then a sharp retest of ₹2,850 with a strong red candle

You realize:
Buyers were not confident — they were greedy.
You short the retest.

Within 30 mins — Reliance drops to ₹2,800.

Reversal Candles = Psychological Signals

You already know the names:

- Hammer
- Shooting Star
- Engulfing
- Doji

But forget the names for now.

Ask this:
"What emotional shift does this candle represent?"

Example:

- Hammer = Panic selling reversed by smart buyers
- Engulfing = Weak bulls/sellers overwhelmed by opposite force
- Doji = Confusion, no commitment

Once you **connect the shape to psychology**,
the market starts speaking to you — not through words, but energy.

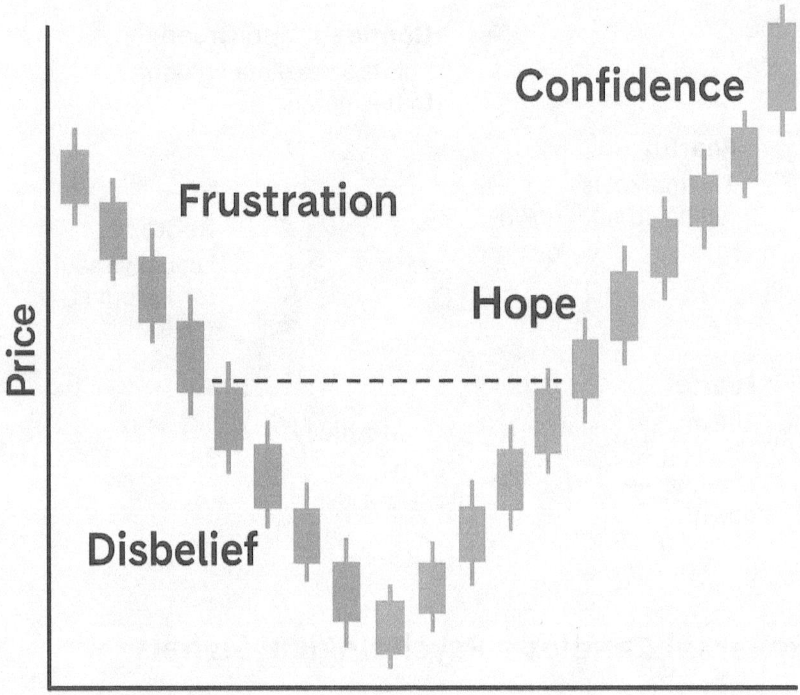

🎯 Action Plan After Chapter 12:

☑ Pick any 2 days on Nifty or BankNifty
☑ For each:

- Mark key support & resistance
- Watch candles at those zones
- Label: Was it hesitation, panic, greed, fakeout?

☑ Screenshot and journal what the **market was feeling** — not just what it did.

☑ Start your **"Candle Psychology Diary"** —
where you don't write entries…
you write emotions.

🧘 Final Mentor Tip:

Most traders learn the chart.
Few learn the mind behind it.

But if you pause before every trade and ask:

> "What emotion is driving this move?"

You will see traps before they're set.
You will ride trends before they explode.
You will exit before the crowd panics.

Because in trading, it's not about what the market is doing.
It's about what people **believe** it's doing.

And when you learn to read that?
You become the sniper.
The silent one.
The one who *feels* the move before it even happens.

Chapter 13

Risk Management Essentials — Survival First

✍ Introduction:

"The best traders are not the best predictors.
They're just the best survivors."

Most people think trading is about big profits, perfect entries, sniper setups.
But the truth?

> **Without risk management, even the best strategy will eventually destroy your account.**

Think of risk management like oxygen.
You don't notice it when it's there.
But the moment it disappears —
you panic, choke, and die.

This chapter is not about being safe.
It's about being **indestructible**.

💣 The Harsh Truth:

> One bad trade, with no stop-loss,
> can undo 20 great trades.

We've all done it.

You take a loss.
You hold on, thinking it'll come back.
It drops further. You add more.
Suddenly you're not trading — you're praying.

Risk management is what separates real traders from emotional gamblers.

📖 Story: The ₹10,000 Revenge

Ravi was having a good month — up ₹9,800.
Then one day, he took a ₹3,000 loss on BankNifty.

He wanted to "make it back."

Next trade: Overleveraged.
Wrong side. Another loss.
This time? No SL.

By EOD, he'd lost ₹12,000.
Not because of his system —
but because he didn't protect himself from himself.

Account Curve Before and After Revenge Trade

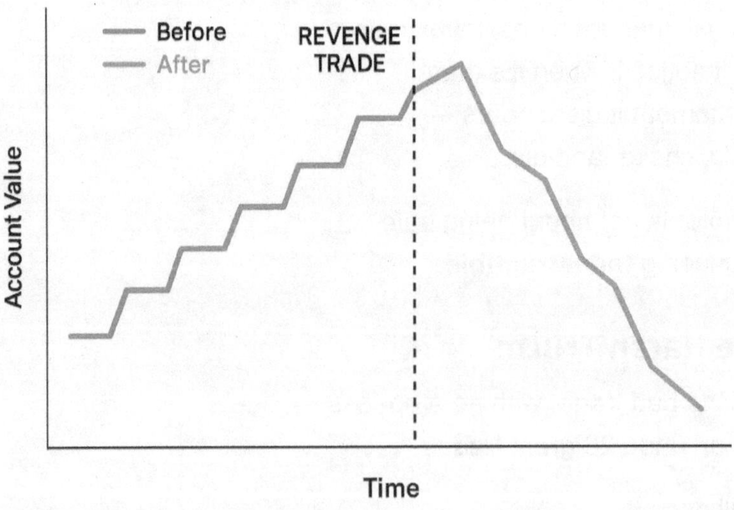

🧠 Core Rule: Risk Per Trade = Always Defined

Before you hit **Buy** or **Sell**, you should already know:

- What is my **maximum loss** if I'm wrong?
- Where is my **exit**, not just my entry?

✅ Professional traders risk **1% or less** of capital per trade.
✅ New traders should aim for **0.5% to 0.75% max**.

Why?

Because you can survive a string of 5–6 losses without damage.
But if you're risking 5% per trade?
You'll be dead in 3 wrong trades.

🧮 The Simple Math That Saves Your Career

Let's say your account = ₹50,000
You decide to risk 1% per trade = ₹500 max loss

You find a setup with:

- SL = ₹10
- Target = ₹20
- RR = 1:2

That means you can trade 50 quantity.

If you're right? You make ₹1,000.
If you're wrong? You lose ₹500.

Now repeat this setup 100 times with discipline.
Even at 50% win-rate, you come out ahead.

This is not trading by emotion.
This is trading by math.

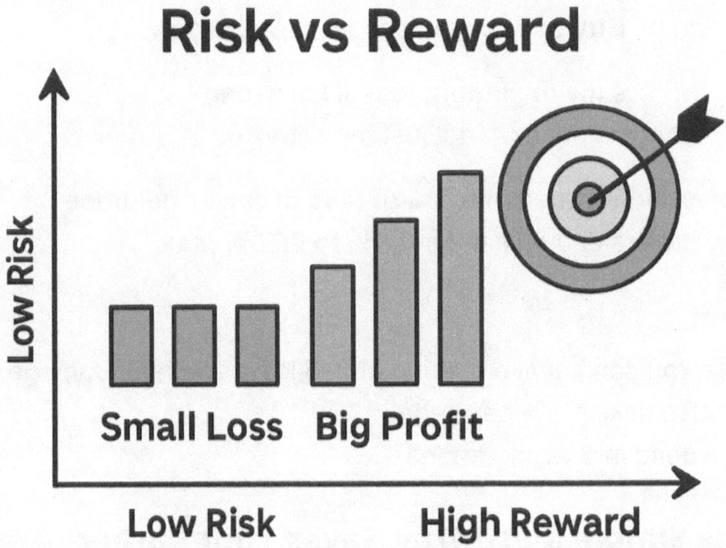

🔐 Stop-Loss is Not Optional. Ever.

"But what if it hits my SL and then comes back?"

That's the voice of fear.
Of regret.
Of fantasy.

The SL is your seatbelt.
You don't wear it because you plan to crash.
You wear it because you know crashes happen.

Smart traders don't remove SLs.
They **respect** them.

SL is not your enemy.
It's your **bodyguard**.

🎯 The 3-Part Risk Management Checklist

1. **Capital Risked per Trade**

   → Max 1% of total capital

2. **Risk-to-Reward Ratio**

   → Aim for 1:1.5 or better

3. **Stop Placement**

   → Logical, not emotional
   → Below structure, not random numbers

📖 Story: Kirti's Comeback

Kirti blew her first account in 6 weeks.
She was skilled, but overconfident.

She restarted with ₹20,000 — and a new rule:

> "I'll never risk more than ₹150 on any trade."

She stayed consistent.
No FOMO. No revenge.
Three months later? ₹36,000.

Not because of better setups.
But because she finally played defense.

Common Trading Mistakes

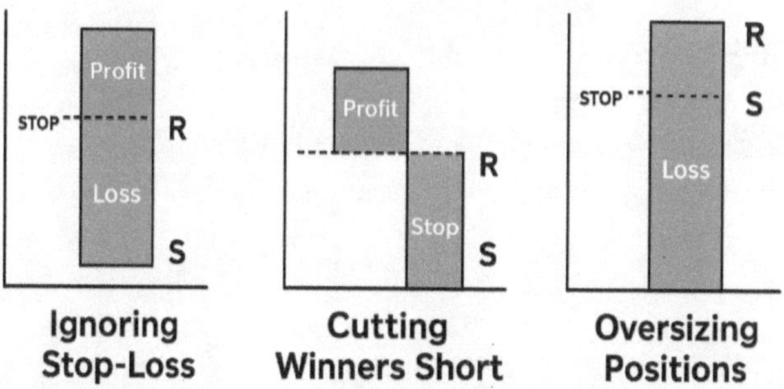

🎯 Action Plan After Chapter 13:

✅ Set your fixed risk per trade (% or ₹)
✅ Backtest 10 trades with proper SL and RR
✅ Track your:

- Win-rate
- Average risk
- Average reward
- Worst-case loss

✅ Build a system around **risk first, profits second**

🧘 Final Mentor Tip:

You don't need to win every battle.
You just need to survive the war.

Most traders blow up not because they're dumb —
but because they risked too much when things didn't work.

Trading is not about being right.
It's about being **prepared when you're wrong.**

So before you ask,

> "Where should I enter?"

First ask:

> "How much can I afford to lose if I'm wrong?"

That single question...
can save your entire career.

Chapter 14

Position Sizing Secrets — How Pros Bet Small & Win Big

✍ Introduction:

"It's not just how good your trade is.
It's how big you bet — and when."

Ask any professional trader:

> "What's the #1 difference between amateurs and pros?"
> Most won't say strategy.
> Most won't say indicators.

They'll say: **position sizing.**

Because if your size is too small,
your wins are meaningless.
If your size is too big,
your losses will crush you emotionally and financially.

Position sizing is what gives traders the **freedom to trade with clarity** —
without fear, greed, or regret.

Let's learn how to size up like a sniper. 🎯

🧠 What Is Position Sizing?

Position sizing = **how much quantity you buy or sell in a trade**.

It's not random.

It's not based on how "sure" you feel.

It's based on:

- Your total capital
- Your risk tolerance
- Your stop-loss distance

It's a **math decision**, not an emotional one.

📖 Story: The "All In" Disaster

Arjun had ₹40,000 in his account.
He saw a strong BankNifty breakout, felt confident.
He went "full margin" — 2 lots.
SL was ₹60.

Guess what?
One red candle — SL hit — he lost ₹6,000 in 3 minutes.
15% of his account, gone.

Same day, same chart —
a pro trader entered 1 lot with perfect sizing.
SL hit? Meh. It was just ₹800.
Next trade? Full recovery + profit.

The difference wasn't skill.
It was **sizing**.

Impact of Overleveraged vs Proper Sizing

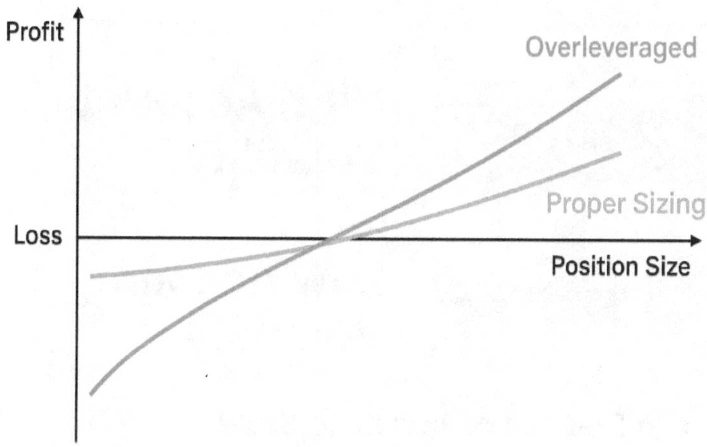

🧮 How to Calculate Position Size (Sniper Style)

Formula:

Position Size = (Risk Amount) ÷ (Stop-Loss Distance)

Example:

- Capital = ₹50,000
- Risk per trade = 1% = ₹500
- SL = ₹10

→ You can buy **50 quantity**

This way:

- Loss = ₹10 × 50 = ₹500 max
- Profit potential = based on your RR
- Emotion = stable, because risk is planned

Max Risk Per Trade

2% Risk	High Account Volatility
0.5% Risk	Low Account Volatility

🧠 When to Reduce or Increase Size?

☑ **Reduce Size If:**

- SL is wide
- Volatility is high
- You're in a losing streak
- Market is uncertain

☑ **Increase Size If:**

- SL is tight
- Setup is A+
- Trend + indicator + price action all align
- You're in sync with market mood

But even then — increase size **gradually, not emotionally.**

📖 Story: The Controlled Bet That Paid Off

Kirti was on a 3-trade win streak.
She saw her favorite pattern forming in Tata Motors.
Instead of going double size,
she increased her lot size by 25% only.
Same rules. Same discipline.

Trade worked.
She booked ₹3,100 profit.

She didn't swing for the fences.
She **grew her risk like a professional**.

🎯 **Action Plan After Chapter 14:**

✅ Calculate your current max risk per trade (1% or less)
✅ Build a simple size formula based on SL size
✅ Test 10 trades using proper sizing
✅ Track:

- Emotional impact
- Recovery speed
- Profit consistency

✅ Write your own rule:

> "I will size based on math, not mood."

🧘 **Final Mentor Tip:**

Position sizing is your risk translator.
It tells the market:
'I respect the game — but I'm here to win long-term.'

You don't need to go big.
You just need to go **consistent**.

Because in trading, it's not about how fast you grow…
It's about how long you last.

Trade small.
Trade smart.
Grow big.

Chapter 15

Trading Journals and Self-Review — Becoming Your Own Coach

✍ Introduction:

"The best trader in your life... is your future self.
Your journal is the map to find them."

Here's the truth:
Most traders chase better entries.
But pros chase better **self-awareness**.

> "Why did I take this trade?"
> "What did I feel before I clicked?"
> "Did I follow my rules, or was I reacting?"

You won't find these answers in indicators.
You'll find them in your **journal**.

This chapter teaches you how to create a self-review system that turns every trade — win or lose — into a **lesson that levels you up.**

What Is a Trading Journal?

It's not a diary.
It's not a spreadsheet with just P&L.

A real trading journal captures:

- What you saw
- What you planned
- What you executed
- How you felt
- What you'll change

It's part **log**, part **mirror**, part **coach**.

📖 Story: The Silent Habit That Changed Everything

Tabrez was a good trader. Sharp setups.
But his equity curve was flat. Random wins and losses.

Then one month, he journaled every single trade.

Patterns emerged:

- Losses happened after back-to-back winners
- Risk increased after big green days
- Most mistakes happened after 11:30 AM

He made **one rule** based on his journal:

> "No new trades after 11:30 unless it's a confirmed A+ setup."

Next month?
Cleaner curve. Fewer losses. Higher confidence.

He didn't change his strategy.
He just became his **own observer.**

Sample Trade Journal Entry

Setup	VWAP Bounce
Date	Apr 12, 2024
Timeframe	5-min
Entry	198.50
Exit	202.80
Result	Gain + 4.30 | Risk-Reward 2.1
Emotion	Calm before, proud after
Notes	Waited for clear bullish candle near VWAP. Quick pop to target. Solid trade.

🧮 What to Log in Your Journal (Sniper Format)

Section	What to Write
Setup Name	Example: VWAP Bounce, Fib Reversal
Timeframe	5-min, 15-min, 1-hour
Entry / Exit	Price, time, screenshot (if possible)
SL / Target	Where & why
Risk/Reward	R-multiple
Emotion Before	Excited, calm, unsure, revengey?
Emotion After	Regret? Pride? Clarity?
Mistake (if any)	Late entry? Poor size? No SL?
Lesson	What to repeat / what to avoid

This turns every trade into a **lesson loop**.

Self-Review

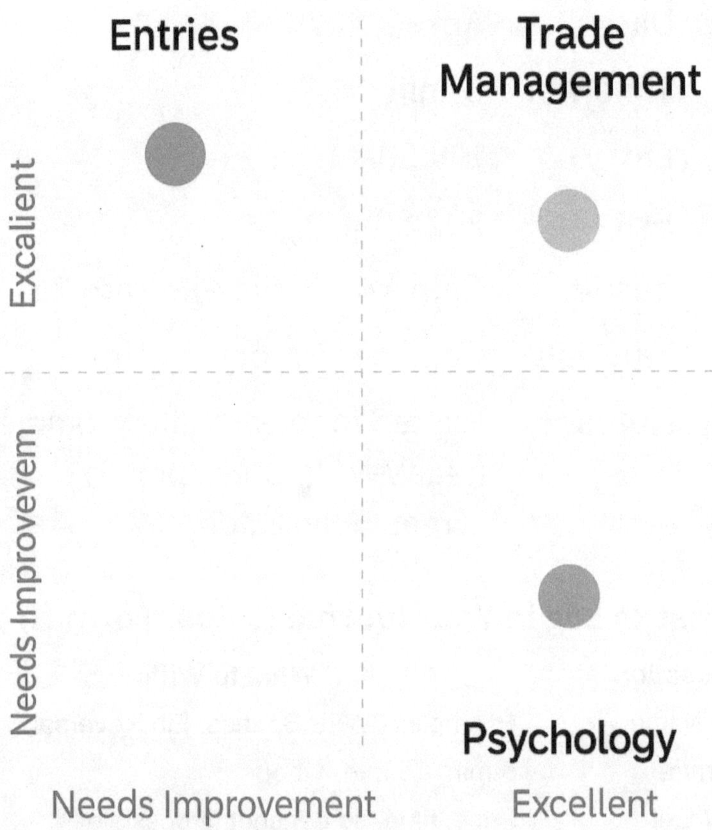

🔁 Weekly + Monthly Self Review

At the end of each week/month:

- Revisit your top 3 wins
- Revisit your top 3 losses

- Note:
  - What patterns helped you win?
  - What emotions caused your losses?
  - Were losses based on logic or impulse?

“Improvement doesn’t come from more trades.
It comes from better reflections.”

🕮 Story: The 30-Day Game Changer

Yashika challenged herself:

> “No matter what happens, I’ll review every trade this month.”

The result?

- She found her top 2 best setups
- Cut out 3 emotional patterns
- Increased her RR from 1:1 to 1:2.3
- Confidence: next level

No guru.
No extra screen time.
Just 30 days of **honest self-coaching**.

**WEEKLY REVIEW SUMMARY CHART–
WINS, MISTAKES, ADJUSTMENTS**

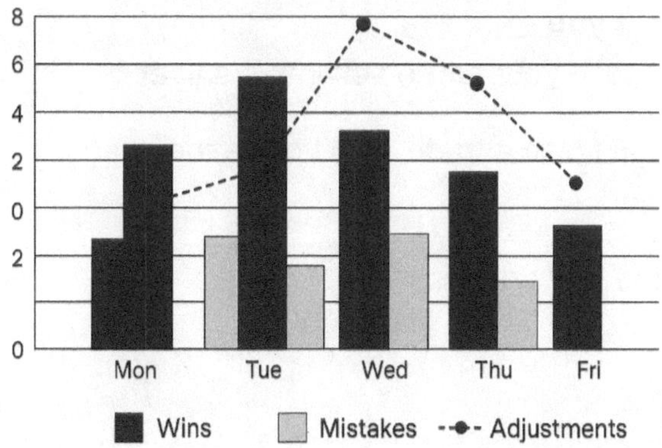

🎯 Action Plan After Chapter 15:

✅ Create a simple journal format (Excel, Notion, Tally, physical — your call)
✅ Log 10 trades in full detail
✅ End each week with:

- What worked
- What didn't
- What you're changing

✅ Set calendar reminder:
"Weekly review = Saturday, 7 PM. Non-negotiable."

🧘 Final Mentor Tip:

The market is not your enemy.
Your memory is.

You think you'll remember that emotional trade.
You won't.
You think you'll remember that perfect breakout entry.
You won't.

But your journal will.

It won't lie to you.
It won't flatter you.
It will just **reflect you** —
and help you coach your future self into a sniper.

So next time you finish a trade, don't close the chart.
Open the journal.

That's where the real edge is.

Chapter 16

Designing Your Trading System — From Random to Reliable

✍ Introduction:

"Traders chase strategies.
Winners build systems."

Every day, millions of traders jump into the market with energy, indicators, and enthusiasm.
But very few walk in with a **system**.

They might know:

- A few patterns
- A couple of indicators
- Some YouTube strategy that worked once

But here's the problem:
They don't have rules.
They don't have structure.
They don't know what to do when their emotions kick in.

That's where most traders fail — **not because of poor setups, but because of poor systems**.

This chapter is about building the **invisible engine** behind your success —
a system that lets you trade calmly, clearly, and consistently.

🧠 What Is a Trading System?

A trading system is more than a strategy.
It's the full framework that answers:

- *What will you trade?*
- *When will you trade it?*
- *How much will you risk?*
- *What confirms a valid setup?*
- *When will you exit — win or lose?*
- *And how will you review to improve?*

Without this, you're just gambling with a keyboard.
With this, you become a process-driven sniper.

📖 Story: The Two Traders at 9:20 AM

Same day. Same market.
Two traders open their charts.

Ravi scans 20 stocks. Sees a breakout. Jumps in. No clear SL. No risk defined.
His mind is racing.

Shreya opens her one-pager system:

> "Only trade VWAP bounce.
> Entry on candle close + volume.
> Max 1% risk per trade.
> No trades after 11:30 AM."

She checks Nifty. Setup aligns. Enters. SL fixed. Target defined.
She executes, logs it, and walks away.

Who's going to last in this game?

Not the one with more setups.
The one with a **system that protects her from herself**.

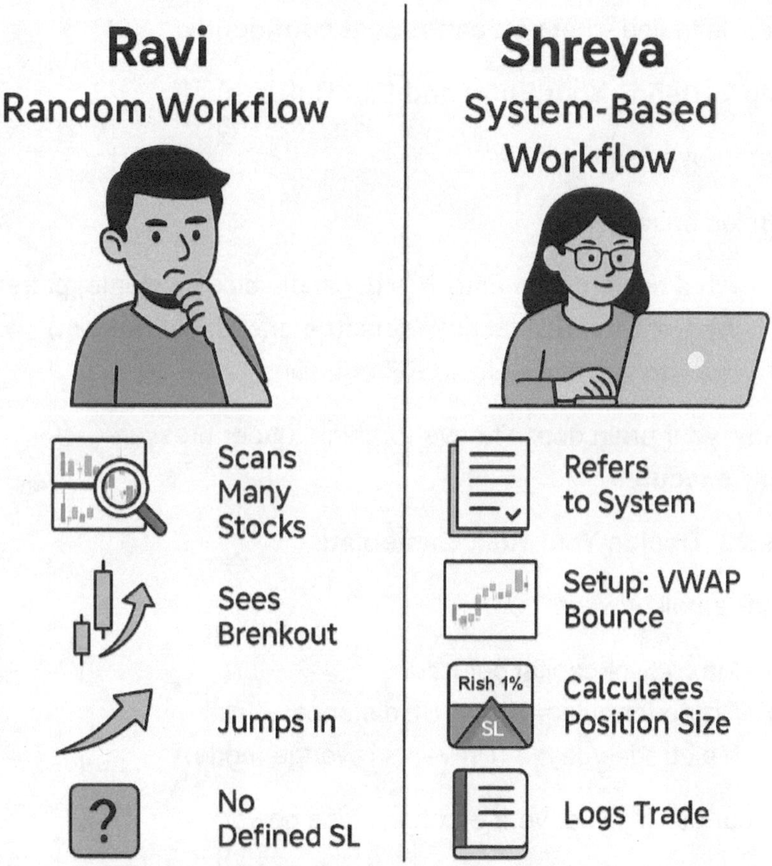

📗 Building Your System: Step-by-Step (With Real Logic)

◈ Step 1: Choose Your Edge

Don't trade everything.
Pick 1–2 setups that suit you.

Examples:

- VWAP + EMA bounce
- Flag breakout after trendline hold
- RSI divergence near support zones

The goal isn't to find a holy grail.
The goal is to find what **you can repeat confidently.**

◈ Step 2: Define Your Entry and Exit Rules

Clarity removes emotion.

Good rules answer:

- What confirms the entry? (e.g. candle close, volume, pattern)
- Where is the SL placed? (structure-based, not random)
- How do you exit — fixed RR or trailing?

This way, your brain doesn't have to "think" under pressure.
It simply **executes**.

◈ Step 3: Decide Your Risk Gameplan

Pros risk small. Always.

- Max 1% of capital per trade
- Sizing formula = Risk ÷ SL distance
- Max trades/day: 3 (Prevents revenge mode)

Once your risk is fixed, your emotions lose power.

◈ Step 4: Create a Trade Routine

> "Discipline is easier when your day has a flow."

Example:

- 9:00 AM – Mark key levels
- 9:15–10:45 AM – Scan setups
- 11:30 AM – Stop if no clean trades
- Post-market – Review & log

This becomes your **trading rhythm**.
No more chaos. Just process.

◈ Step 5: Feedback Loop — Your Growth Engine

A system is useless without review.

Each weekend:

- Review top 3 wins
- Review top 3 losses
- Track win%, average RR, setup success rate
- Refine system **once a month**, not every day

This is how your system gets **smarter than you**.

📖 Story: The Sticky Note System

Latika was tired of overtrading.
She created a 5-line system and stuck it on her laptop.

1. Only VWAP + EMA bounce
2. Entry: Green 5-min candle above VWAP + volume
3. SL = below structure
4. Risk = ₹300
5. Max 2 trades/day

She followed it without fail.

Result?
Less confusion.
More consistency.
She didn't need more tools. She just needed better **rules.**

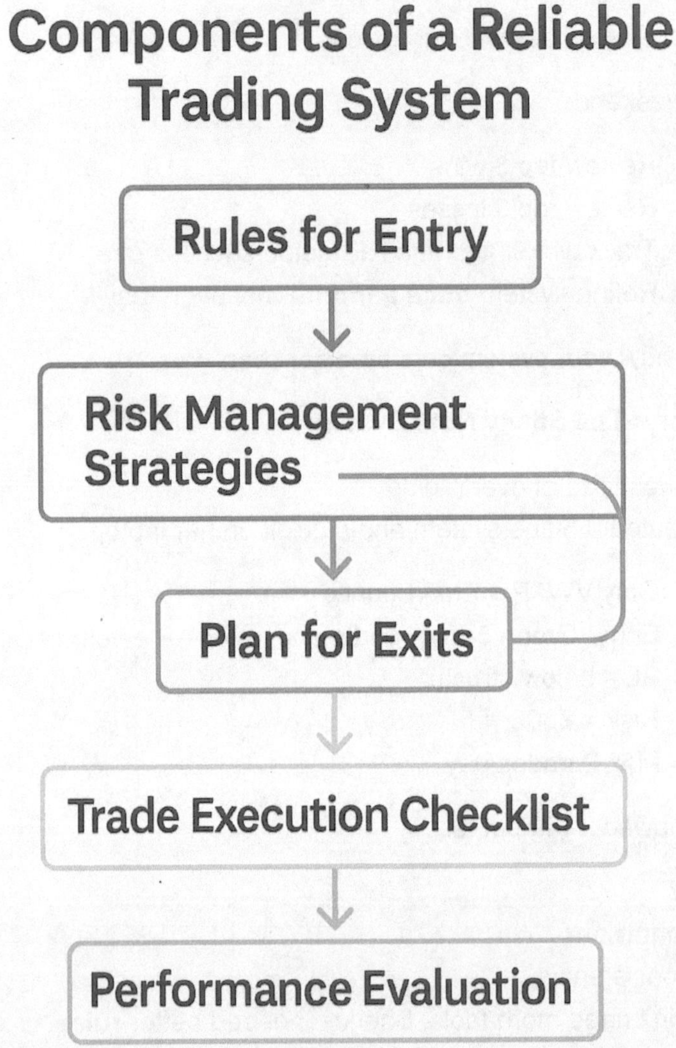

🧭 The Power of Testing Before Tinkering

Here's where most traders fail:

They tweak their system **after 1 loss**.
They panic and say: "It's not working!"

Pro tip:

> Don't judge your system until you've tested it across 30–50 trades.

Let data guide your changes — not your feelings.

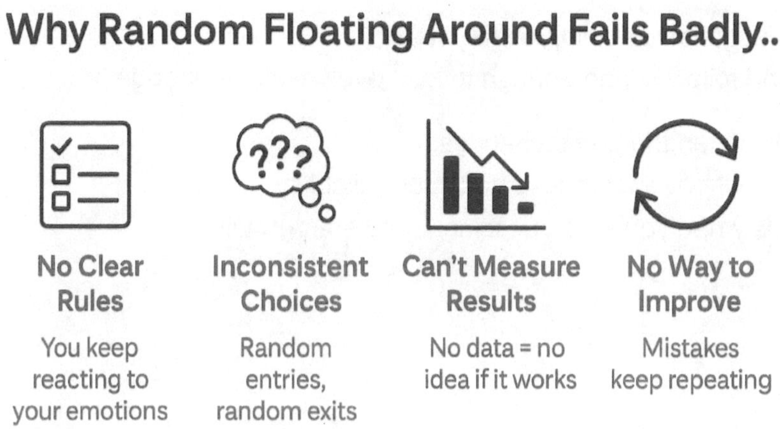

🎯 Action Plan After Chapter 16:

✅ Choose 2 high-confidence setups
✅ Write your entry/exit/risk rules
✅ Commit to a daily routine
✅ Create a one-page "My System" visual
✅ Print it. Stick it. Follow it for 30 trades

> After 30 trades → Review. Refine. Repeat.

This is how consistency is built.

🧘 Final Mentor Tip:

If you can't explain your system in one minute, you don't have a system — you have chaos.

Your system is your boss when the market gets noisy.
It's your anchor when your emotions rise.
It's your mirror when things go wrong.

And the beauty?

You don't need to build the perfect system.

You just need to build **your system**
— and follow it long enough to let it evolve into your edge.

That's when the game changes.
That's when randomness becomes reliability.
That's when you stop guessing... and start growing.

Chapter 17

Handling Winning and Losing Streaks — Emotional Mastery

✍ Introduction:

"Markets don't destroy traders.
Overconfidence and despair do."

Every trader, no matter how skilled, goes through streaks.

You might be:

- On fire — three green days in a row
- Or stuck — four stop-loss hits back-to-back

What separates long-term winners from weekend warriors?
Not better indicators.
Not bigger bets.

But the ability to **handle emotional momentum** — both positive and negative — without letting it hijack your system.

📈 The Psychology of Streaks

Think of trading like a rhythm.
Sometimes you're flowing with it.
Sometimes you're forcing it.

Both **winning streaks** and **losing streaks** are traps —
because they change how you think:

▲ The Winning Streak Trap

- You feel unstoppable
- You increase size too fast
- You skip rules
- You think the market "owes" you

This is when the **ego enters silently** — and often ends the party.

🕮 Story: Mohit's Overconfidence Blow-Up

Mohit nailed 4 trades in 2 days.
He doubled his position size on the fifth.
No stop-loss. "I can't be wrong."

He was wrong.

Lost ₹7,800 in 6 minutes.
Wiped half of the week's gains — and mentally broke down.

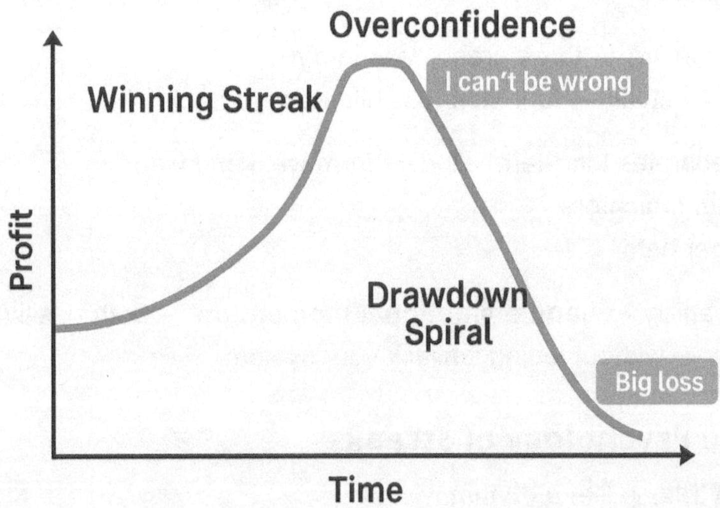

▼ The Losing Streak Trap

- You start doubting your system
- You force revenge trades

- You change strategies mid-week
- You shrink risk too much — then miss the comeback trade

Losing streaks don't just hurt your capital.
They **crack your belief**.

📖 Story: Aditi's 3-Day Freeze

Aditi lost 3 trades in a row.
She stopped taking valid trades after that — too scared.
Missed her favorite setup on the fourth day — which worked beautifully.

She realized:

> "The losing didn't kill me.
> My fear of losing again did."

🧠 How to Handle Winning Streaks Like a Pro

☑ Reduce size after 3 big wins — keep your balance
☑ Stick to exact rules — no "gut calls"
☑ Journal emotions, not just trades
☑ Take a break for 1 session after huge days — reset ego

The goal is **not to ride the high** — it's to **protect your edge**.

🧘 How to Handle Losing Streaks Like a Sniper

☑ Go back to smallest size
☑ Only take your A+ setup
☑ Stop trading if mind is noisy
☑ Read your best journaled trades
☑ Remind yourself: Losing streaks = part of math, not a signal of failure

The market didn't change.
You just need to **reconnect with your process**.

📖 Story: Kirti's "Reset Week" Rule

After every 4 SLs in a row, she switches to:

- Paper trading
- Chart backtesting
- Watching price action silently

It's not quitting.
It's **resetting**.

Next week, she returns sharper — like an athlete after a recharge.

🎯 Action Plan After Chapter 17:

☑ Write your rule for winning streak:

"If I win 3 trades in a row, I will _____."

☑ Write your rule for losing streak:

"If I lose 3 trades in a row, I will _____."

☑ Create a "Mental Reset Checklist":

- Step away
- Review top 5 best trades
- Watch 3 charts without trading
- Meditate / walk / reset state

Stick this checklist near your screen.
Because mental health is trading capital too.

🧘 Final Mentor Tip:

You don't rise by avoiding streaks.
You rise by staying balanced through them.

Markets test your system.
But streaks test your **soul**.

> When you win, stay humble.
> When you lose, stay present.
> When you feel lost — return to process.

This is what builds long-term consistency.
This is what separates the snipers from the survivors.

You're not here for one big win.
You're here for the long game.

So play it like a pro.

❁

Chapter 18

Advanced Patterns – Flags, Wedges, and Pro-Level Setups

✍ Introduction:

"Not every breakout is a real move.
But some patterns speak the language of smart money."

As a trader evolves, they start seeing that markets **move in waves** —
Sharp impulse, followed by clean pause.
Aggression → Consolidation → Continuation.

That pause? That structure?
It's where flags and wedges are born.

Most retail traders try to trade patterns based on looks.
But pros know that **context + confirmation** is what makes an advanced pattern truly powerful.

In this chapter, we decode:

- Flag patterns
- Pennants
- Rising & falling wedges
- and the sniper-level way to trade them

🏁 Flag Patterns — The Calm Before the Storm

What it is:

A **flag** is a pause in a trend — usually a small pullback after a big move.

- Price rallies fast
- Then forms a **channel-like drift** in the opposite direction
- Looks like a mini flag waving on a pole

This is **not a reversal.** It's a **breather**.

> When a flag forms after strong momentum, it usually breaks **in the direction of the trend.**

📖 Story: The BankNifty Flag Trap

Price moved up 300 points in 20 mins.
Then drifted slowly down for the next 30 mins, forming a falling channel.

Most traders got scared.
You? You spotted the flag.

As soon as a bullish candle broke out of the flag — with volume — you entered.
Target? The height of the flagpole.

Reward? ₹120 in 10 minutes.

You didn't chase.
You read the pattern. Then you struck.

📌 Wedges — The Tightening Coil

A **wedge** forms when price compresses between two angled trendlines.

- **Falling Wedge** = Bullish reversal
- **Rising Wedge** = Bearish reversal

Key idea:

> Price gets squeezed tighter... until it explodes out.

How to Trade Wedges:

- Draw clear converging trendlines
- Wait for breakout **with volume**
- Entry = candle close outside wedge
- SL = inside the wedge (last swing)
- Target = height of widest part of wedge

🕮 Story: Reliance's Falling Wedge

Reliance was downtrending for 2 days.
On day 3, price formed lower highs, but sellers were getting weaker.
A clean falling wedge formed.

Breakout + bullish engulfing candle + volume pop
→ You enter.

Stock rallied ₹18 in 30 minutes.
You caught the turn — because you didn't just see price…
You saw **pressure building**.

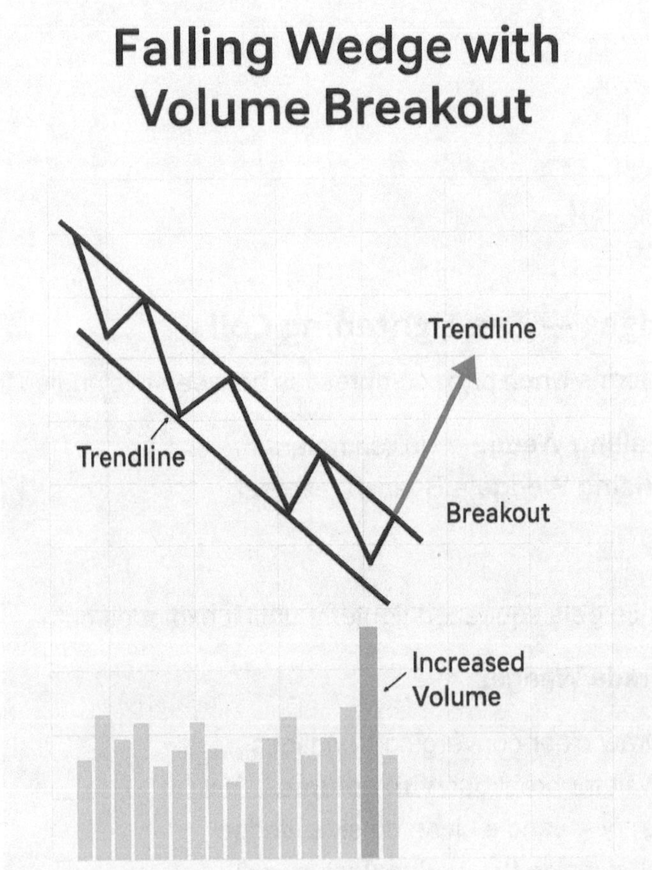

🔥 Bonus Setup — Pennants and Explosive Continuations

Think of a **pennant** like a flag — but tighter and more triangular.
It looks like a mini symmetrical triangle after a fast move.

Used especially in intraday breakouts (Nifty, BankNifty, high-beta stocks)

📌 Setup Logic:

- Big impulse candle
- Price goes into a tiny symmetrical squeeze
- Breakout confirms continuation

This setup has **low risk and high speed** when traded correctly.

📖 **Story: Tata Motors Intraday Pennant**

After a news-based breakout, Tata Motors surged 4%.
You didn't chase the spike.

You waited.

Price coiled into a tight pennant.
You entered on breakout + VWAP support.

The next candle? ₹6 rally in 3 mins.
No tension.
No guessing.
Just sniper confirmation.

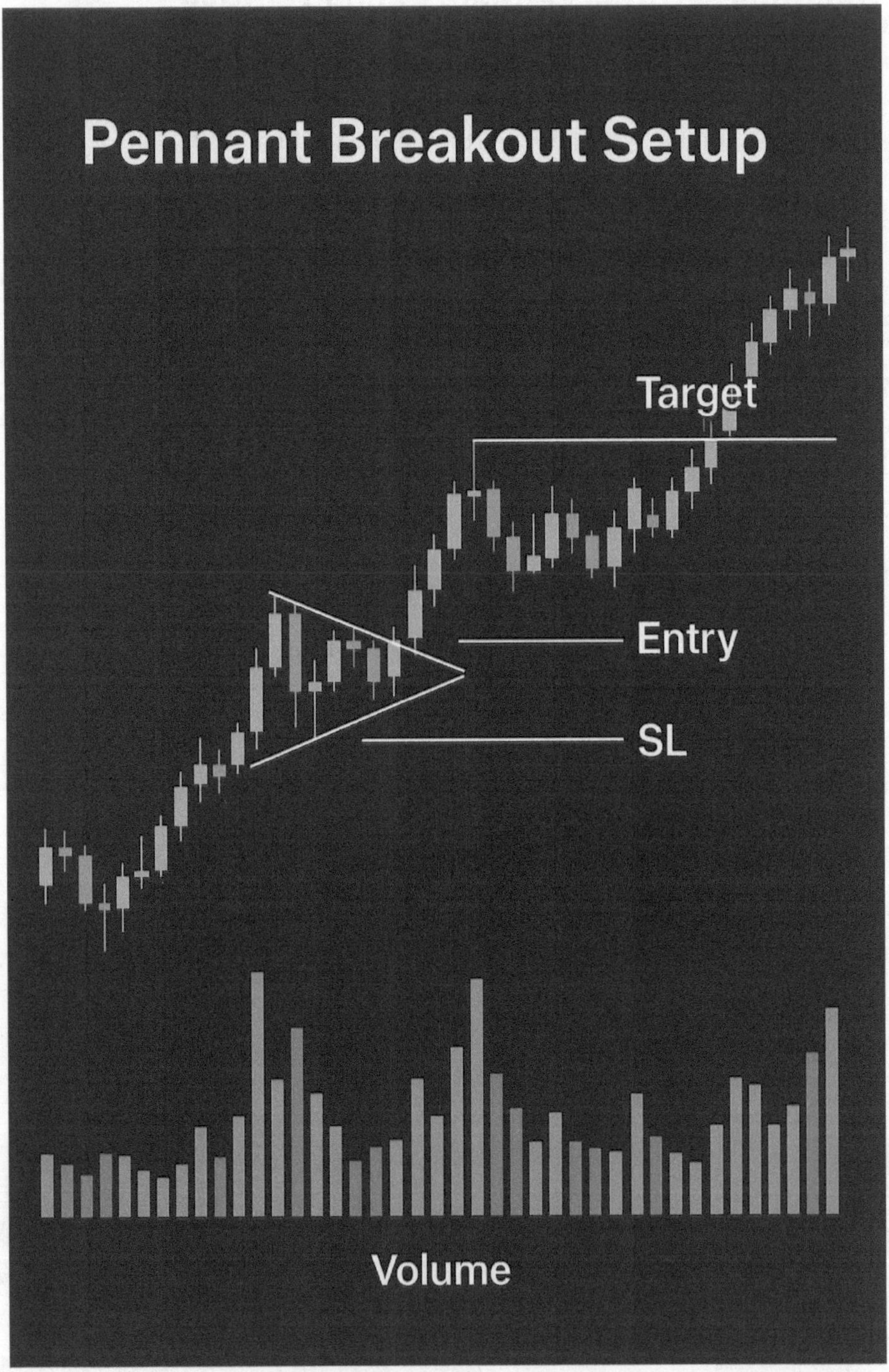
Pennant Breakout Setup
Target
Entry
SL
Volume

🧠 Key Rules for Advanced Pattern Trading:

☑ Always trade **with volume** — patterns without volume are weak
☑ Flag & pennant = continuation
☑ Wedge = potential reversal
☑ Setups work best **when the trend was strong before the pattern**
☑ SL must be **within the pattern** — tight but logical
☑ Only trade the breakout — never predict

> "You don't anticipate explosions. You prepare for them and trigger on confirmation."

🎯 Action Plan After Chapter 18:

☑ Practice drawing 3 flag patterns, 2 wedges, 2 pennants on recent Nifty/BankNifty charts
☑ Mark:

- Impulse leg
- Pattern formation
- Entry candle
- SL and expected target

☑ Track which pattern worked best — and in what market conditions
☑ Start building your own "Pattern Playbook"

🧘 Final Mentor Tip:

Patterns are not magic.
They're maps of energy.

They show you where the market breathes.
Where it pauses.
Where smart money is loading.
And where momentum is about to be released.

Your job is not to guess the move —
Your job is to **wait for the pattern to complete its message.**

Because when patterns speak with clarity…
A sniper listens — and acts.

Chapter 19

How to Build a Daily Watchlist — Preparation as an Edge

✍ Introduction:

In the world of trading, it's easy to believe success lies in fast execution, secret indicators, or fancy setups.
But ask any consistently profitable trader their edge, and many will say:

> **"Preparation."**

The market rewards clarity — and punishes noise.
Each morning, the screen opens to chaos. Hundreds of charts. News. Price ticks. Opinions.
And yet, the trader with a prepared watchlist enters the battlefield with calm confidence.
They don't hunt for trades.
They wait for their shortlisted zones to light up.

This chapter is about **building your daily edge — before the first candle forms.**
Because the trade you don't prepare for… is the one that takes more than your money.

🧠 The Problem With "Open the Chart and Decide"

Most traders begin their day the same way:
They open 10–15 random charts at 9:10 AM, scroll fast, react faster, and hope one of them "feels good."

This is not trading.
This is emotional roulette.

Without preparation:

- You enter late
- Your stop-loss is random
- Your mind is distracted
- You exit too early… or too late
- You blame the market for your own fog

"You're not supposed to be searching for the trade at 9:20.
You're supposed to be **executing the plan you built at 8:45.**"

📖 Story: The 2-Hour Chaos That Changed Everything

Mohit had a habit of jumping into the market without a plan.
He'd hop from Tata Motors to Reliance to BankNifty to a small-cap tip from a Telegram group.
Every day felt like a gamble.

One morning, his intraday hit ₹3,200 loss — not because the setup failed,
but because he didn't know **why he entered**. No structure. No prep.

Frustrated, he tried something new.

The next day, he built a 3-stock watchlist —
each with a trigger price, a clean pattern, and one line explaining **why** it was on the list.

At 10:42 AM, his setup triggered.
He entered with confidence. SL hit? Fine. But he was calm.
Why? Because the plan was in place before emotion entered the room.

🧰 What Makes a Great Watchlist

A powerful watchlist is not long. It's precise.
It answers three simple questions:

1. **What are you watching?**
2. **Why is it on your list?**
3. **What will you do if the setup triggers?**

Nothing more.
No guessing. No overthinking.
Just clear, calm preparation.

DAILY WATCHLIST

STOCK	SETUP	TRIGGER	SL	NOTES
RELIANCE	Ascending Triangle	2480	2440	Buy if breaks 2480 on volume
TATA MOTORS	Channel Breakdown	400	412	Sell below 400 support
BANKNIFTY	Pullback to VWAP	39500	39800	Long if holds VWAP

❑ The Craft of Building a Daily Watchlist (Mentor Method)

Start the night before. Or early morning. Doesn't matter.
What matters is rhythm — not randomness.

🕵 Step 1: Scan With Intent

Look at the broader market.
What's trending? Where's the volume flowing?
Are any major stocks at breakout levels? Is there a news-based mover?

Avoid trying to trade everything.
Filter for **5–7 stocks**. That's your battlefield.

✍ Step 2: Open the Charts — One at a Time

Slow down.
Draw support/resistance. Look for patterns. Are EMAs aligned?
Ask yourself: "Would I be confident if this breaks here?"

If the answer is "Maybe"... remove it.
Your list must contain **only setups that make you feel calm.**

🧠 Step 3: Write Your Execution Logic

For each stock you keep, write one simple line:

> "If [trigger level] breaks with volume, I will enter. SL = [logic], Target = [logic]"

For example:

> "If Infosys breaks ₹1,460 on volume, I'll enter. SL below 20EMA. Target near ₹1,475 swing."
> "If BankNifty holds VWAP after 10:15 AM, I'll enter on a bullish candle with volume."

That's it.

Sample Daily Watchlist

Stock	Setup	Trigger	SL	Notes
Infosys	Bullish Flag	₹1,460 breakout	Below flag low	Waiting for breakout
Reliance	Support Bounce	Near ₹2,330	Below support	EMA confirmation
Nifty Bank	VWAP Reclaim	Above VWAP	Below WVAP	Check volume

⚔ What Happens When You Trade Without One

When you trade without a watchlist:

- You enter late and cut early
- You chase FOMO setups that weren't even in your plan
- You trade out of boredom, not logic
- You overtrade because you're reacting, not planning

A sniper doesn't reload mid-shot.
He loads his weapon **before** the fight begins.

📖 Story: The Peace of a Prepared Mind

Yashika once said something that stuck with the team:

> "My best trades feel boring. Because by the time I enter, I've already lived the trade once — in my plan."

That's the mindset we aim for.

No hype.
Just process.

🎯 Action Exercise – Watchlist Warrior Ritual

For the next 5 sessions, try this:

1. Pick your 3 best-looking stocks by 9:05 AM
2. Mark clear levels — trigger, SL, Target
3. Write one line explaining what you'll do
4. Execute ONLY from this list
5. End of day: Review what triggered, what worked, what didn't

Repeat this for a week.
The calm you'll feel will be your **first step into sniper-level focus**.

🧘 Final Mentor Tip:

You don't need 100 options.
You need 3 strong ideas, prepared with intention.

Most traders lose because they show up unprepared —
scrolling, guessing, reacting.

But when you build your list with purpose,
when you start the day with a simple plan…

You become the trader who acts with clarity
— while the rest are still chasing noise.

Trade what you planned.
Ignore what you didn't.
And let the market do the rest.

Chapter 20

How to Think, Act, and Win Like a Market Sniper

Part 5 – 10/10 Trader Blueprint

A Quiet Evolution

At the beginning of your journey, everything felt loud.
The charts. The indicators. The YouTube strategies. The dopamine hits of a green PnL.
You thought the goal was to win.
But now, after all the lessons, all the setups, all the losses and recoveries — you realize something deeper:

> **The real goal is to stay sharp, stay calm, and stay in the game.**

A sniper doesn't look for chaos.
They **wait for clarity**.
They don't react — they **prepare**.
They don't hope — they **trust their system**.

And they never shoot without a plan.

This chapter isn't a strategy. It's a lens.
A lens that shows you what elite traders see — and how they move.

I. Precision Over Prediction

Most traders spend their time predicting what the market will do.

Snipers don't.

They don't need to be right about direction.

They only need to be right about **their moment**.

Here's how their lens is different:

Retail Trader	Market Sniper
Watches 10 charts	Watches 2 high-conviction setups
Changes bias mid-trade	Enters *only* when plan aligns
Asks "Is this a breakout?"	Asks "Does this match my system?"
Trades to feel in control	Trades only when they are in control

The sniper removes the noise, the opinions, the pressure.

They don't just follow a strategy. They operate by **principles**.

> *"If the setup is unclear, the sniper doesn't negotiate. They skip it."*

II. The System Before the Shot

You don't build discipline in the moment — you build it **before** the market opens.
Everything a sniper needs is already decided *before* the first candle prints:

- **Watchlist**: Based on volume, structure, and catalysts
- **Zones marked**: No guessing during price movement
- **Risk pre-decided**: 0.5% to 1% per trade, always
- **SL & TP defined**: Never moved mid-trade

- **Mental state checked**: No trading if anxious, distracted, or tilted

By the time the bell rings, the sniper is not looking for trades.
They're looking for **confirmation** of what they already planned.

And if the confirmation doesn't come?
They do nothing.

And that — is power.

III. Operating the Day: Sniper Execution Flow

Professional trading is not emotional.
It's operational.

Here's what a sniper's day *actually* looks like:

✦ Pre-Market (30–60 min before open)

- Journal entry from the previous day reviewed
- Top 2–3 stocks indexed for volume, narrative, clean structure
- Key levels marked (no more than 3 per chart)
- Alerts set — not eyes glued to the screen
- Trade plan written in simple checklist:
- "If price reaches zone X, forms candle Y, with volume Z — I enter. Else, I don't."

✦ Live Session

- Chart open. Phone silenced. Music off.
- One trade at a time — *no multitasking*
- If entry triggers → size and stop already known
- Trade executed without hesitation
- If stop hits — exit, breathe, *no revenge clicks*
- If target hits — partial out, move SL, let runner go or exit full

✦ Post-Market

- Screenshot taken, labeled (Win/Loss, setup used, emotion score)
- One-sentence journal entry: "Today, I did/did not follow my system because…"
- Platform closed, routine ends.
- Market doesn't enter dinner time, family time, or rest.

"If you treat trading like a job, it can pay you like one. If you treat it like a game, it will punish you every time."

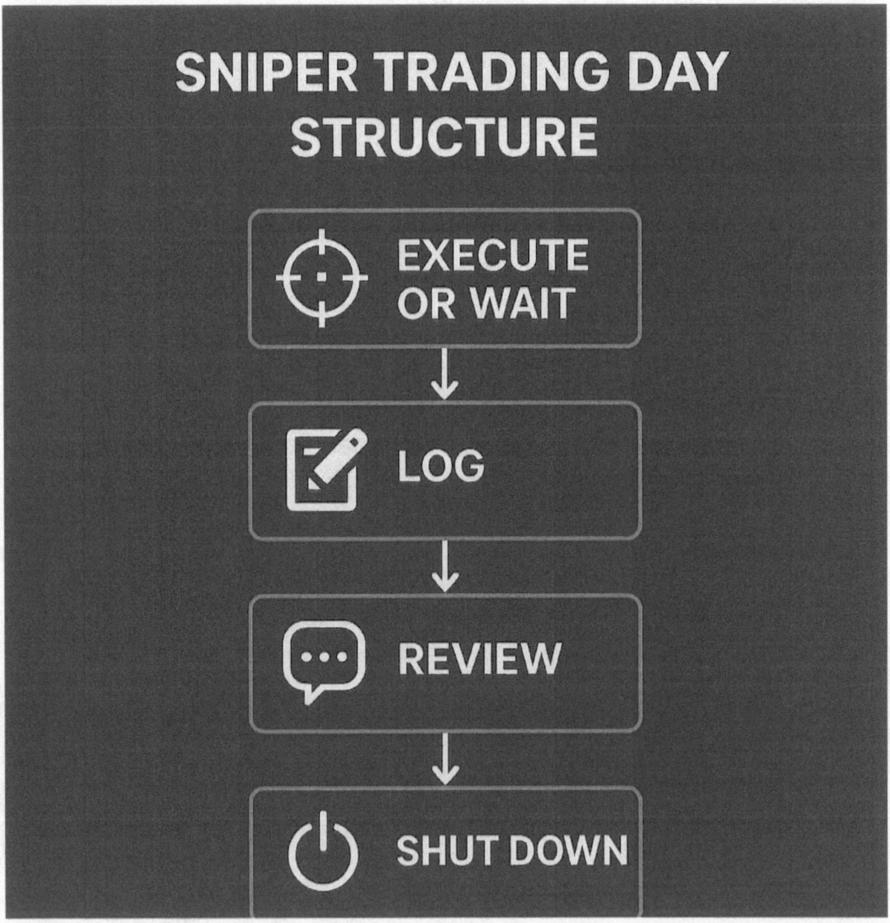

IV. The Psychology of Staying Unshaken

Markets are uncertain.
But your mind doesn't have to be.

What gives a sniper mental strength is not the willpower to "stay strong" — it's the **rules they've already committed to**.

They build mental guardrails:

- *2 trade rule*: After 2 red trades — stop.
- *Maximum loss per day*: Fixed in % — no override.
- *No trade = still a win*: A skipped bad trade is a strategic victory.
- *Post-loss walk*: 5 minutes away from the screen after every stopout.

They don't resist emotion.
They **design around it**.

"A sniper's strength isn't in being fearless. It's in being structured."

V. Winning Without Needing to Win

You know you're evolving when:

- You start aiming for clean setups, not big profits.
- You feel more peace on the sidelines than in random action.
- You value **consistency** over spikes.
- You walk away satisfied even after a zero-trade day.

Snipers don't chase green days.
They chase **clean execution**.
Because they know: when your system is solid, **profit follows behavior** — not the other way around.

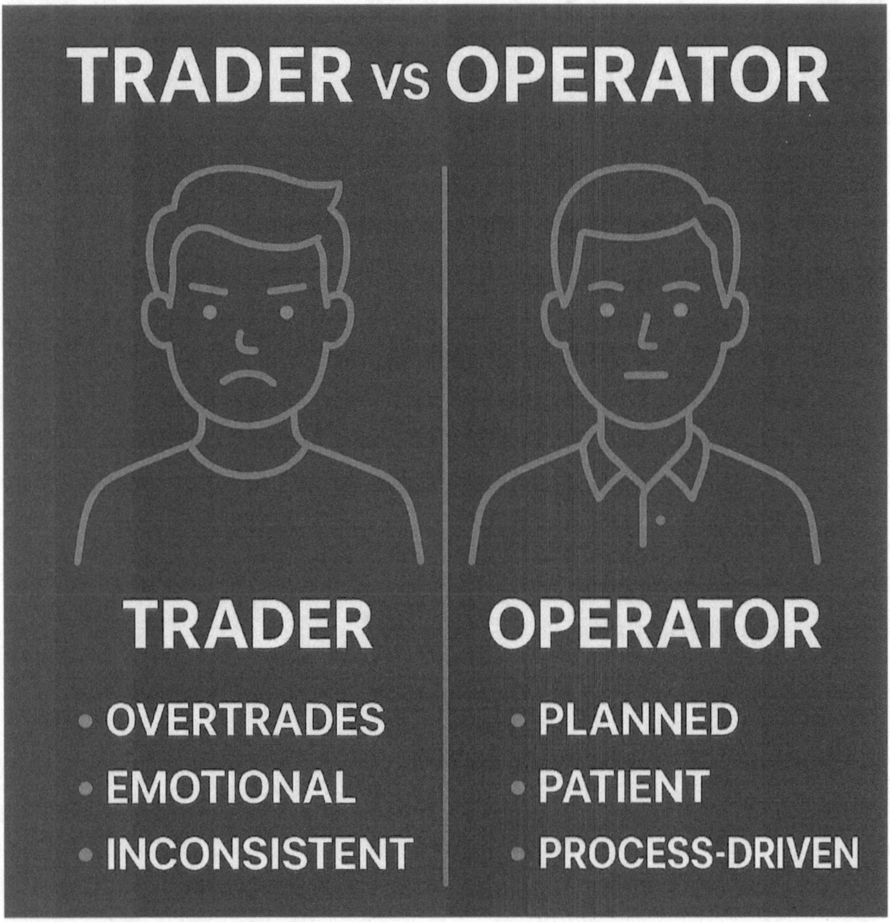

VI. Becoming the Operator

This chapter is called "How to Win," but the real win is this:

> You're no longer trying to trade. You've become someone who's capable of trading **for a lifetime**.

You now operate like a system:

- You enter when conditions match
- You exit based on logic, not panic
- You don't guess — you execute
- You don't need thrill — you need clarity

This is what separates a good trader from a long-term winner: **identity**.

Final Note: The Trader You're Meant to Be

This isn't the end of your learning.
But it is the moment where you stop being a student of theory — and start becoming a **builder of your own edge**.

You don't need another course.
You don't need another guru.
You need time, reflection, structure — and **yourself**.

> You are now your own mentor. Your own system. Your own edge.

Close this book.
Open your chart.
And wait for your shot — not because you're excited.
But because you're **ready**.

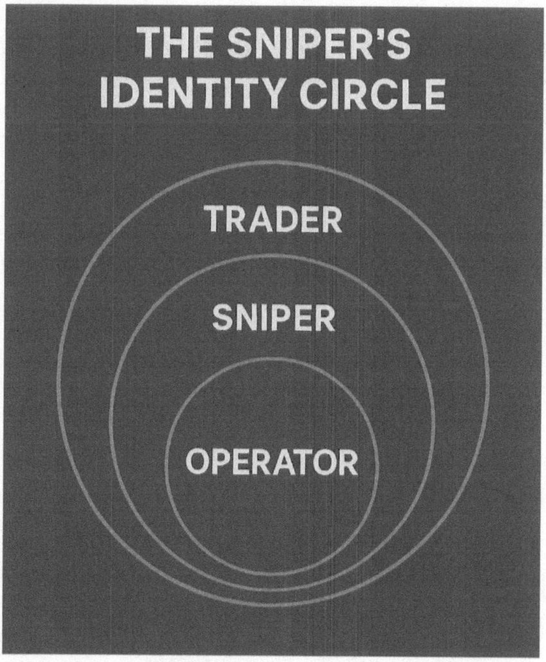

📓 Final Note: This Is Not the End

You've reached the final chapter. But the truth is — this isn't the end. This is where your real trading life begins.

You now know how to think clearly, trade patiently, and act with precision. But consistency doesn't come from knowledge alone. It comes from **repetition**. From showing up. From adjusting without overreacting. From evolving — one clean decision at a time.

You won't need every chapter from this book every day.
But some pages will become lifelong companions.
Some notes will return to you in moments of doubt.
And some lessons will turn into instinct.

There will be losing days.
There will be flat months.
And there will be moments you question everything.
But if you stay calm, stay honest, and stay in flow —
you'll be surprised at how far your system can take you.

This is not the end. It's the start of your next 100 sniper trades.

Close this book.
Open your chart.
And walk forward — one clear shot at a time.

🎁

Bonus 1

40 Pro Tips for Intraday Traders

High-performance habits, tested truths, and sniper-level reminders

These aren't motivational quotes.

These are things elite traders actually follow — quietly, daily.

✅ Entry & Execution

1. Wait for confirmation — not anticipation.
2. Enter on clarity, not speed.
3. Trade what you see, not what you wish.
4. Your best trade of the day may not come. Be okay with that.
5. Size small enough to stay calm — every trade.
6. One setup. One reason. One execution.
7. A late entry on confirmation is better than early regret.
8. The first 15 minutes of the market often lie.

✅ Risk & Capital Protection

9. SL is not optional. Ever.
10. Accept risk *before* clicking "Buy."
11. Daily max loss rule = trader survival kit.
12. Never double size after a loss.
13. Two red trades? Pause. Breathe.
14. Losses are tuition. Expensive when ignored.

15. Small green > forced revenge recovery.
16. Red days are allowed — destruction is not.

☑ Psychology & Self-Control

17. You're not your PnL.
18. Emotional discipline = the rarest edge.
19. Walk away when tilted. Even for 10 minutes.
20. You don't have to win today. You have to last 10 years.
21. Don't react to a candle. Respond to your plan.
22. Journal what *you felt*, not just what you did.
23. No trading when tired, distracted, or emotionally off.
24. Your ego wants to be right. Your account wants to be small and smart.

☑ Chart & Setup Filters

25. Trade clean charts — no chaos, no clutter.
26. High-volume + strong structure > anything.
27. Candle + volume tells the truth.
28. Gaps, news, and earnings matter — plan accordingly.
29. If it's not in your sniper plan — skip it.
30. Don't invent new setups mid-session.
31. One timeframe for entry. Higher for confirmation.

☑ Lifestyle & Longevity

32. Trade fewer setups, master them deeply.
33. No social media during live session. Period.
34. Avoid backtesting paralysis — forward test with care.
35. Sleep is a trading tool.
36. Breathe before every session.
37. Log out after your window — protect your peace.
38. Learn from one mentor, not ten gurus.
39. Rest days are performance enhancers.
40. You don't have to trade to be a trader.

Bonus 2

The Daily Pre-Market Checklist

Start your session like a sniper, not a spectator

> A sniper never enters the field unprepared.
> Neither should you.

Use this checklist every morning to build consistency and mental calm before you enter the charts.

✅ 1. Mindset Check (Before Screens)

- Did I sleep at least 6–7 hours?
- Am I emotionally neutral — not hyped, not tilted?
- Can I afford to lose 1–2R today without it affecting my mood or mindset?
- Quick breathwork (1 minute inhale–hold–exhale)
- Reminder: *You don't need to trade today. Only if your setup appears.*

✅ 2. Journal Review (5-Minute Lookback)

- Did I follow my system yesterday?
- Was my last trade clean or emotional?
- What is *one key learning* I carry into today?

✅ 3. News & Events Scan

- Global sentiment check: US, Asia, EU markets
- India news / events / earnings calendar

- Is today high-volatility? (e.g., RBI, inflation, Nifty expiry?)
- Avoid new setups 15 mins before/after major news

☑ 4. Watchlist Refinement

- Pick **2–3 top setups** — not more
- Mark clean S/R zones on chart
- Identify current trend and key volume areas
- Set alerts — *don't babysit candles*

☑ 5. Trade Setup Conditions

- Entry condition clearly defined?
- *("If price breaks X with volume Y, then entry at Z")*
- Stoploss pre-defined — no mental stops
- Risk % locked (0.5–1% per trade)
- Targets calculated (based on structure, not dreams)

☑ 6. Trading Environment

- Notifications silenced (phone, apps, DND mode ON)
- Distraction-free desk setup
- Chart layout clean — only essential indicators
- Remind yourself: *Watch. Wait. Don't force.*

"A professional day begins before the market does."

This checklist is your edge — don't skip it.

⚠

Bonus 3

Mistakes to Avoid in 2026–27 Volatile Markets

Hard truths, tactical reminders, and system-killers to sidestep

Volatility creates opportunity — but it also magnifies every bad habit.
The traders who survive are the ones who stop making these mistakes.

✕ 1. Overtrading in Hyper-Volatility

- The market is moving fast — but that doesn't mean you should.
- Choppy range = SL factory.
- *Solution:* Trade smaller size. Wait for full confirmation. Fewer, cleaner entries.

✕ 2. Trading Without Context

- No news check. No event calendar. Just vibes.
- Suddenly, you're stuck mid-trade during RBI policy or global panic.
- *Solution:* Always check calendar + news. Protect your capital from surprises.

✕ 3. Improvising Your Setup Mid-Session

- You planned a breakout. But now you're "feeling" a bounce.
- Market tricks your emotions — you end up with no clarity and full risk.
- *Solution:* Write your setup conditions before market opens. Follow only that.

✕ 4. Ignoring Volume Confirmation

- In volatility, **volume is your truth-teller**.
- Breakouts without volume? Fakeouts.
- Pullbacks on low volume? Weak conviction.
- *Solution:* Combine price + volume every time. It's non-negotiable.

✕ 5. Forcing Trades on Non-Trending Days

- Not every day has a clean move.
- Volatility doesn't mean direction — it means chaos too.
- *Solution:* Accept zero-trade days. They're part of being a sniper.

✕ 6. Widening Stoploss "Just This Once"

- Volatility hits SL? You think, "Next time I'll give it more room."
- That "room" becomes destruction.
- *Solution:* Respect your stop. Shrink position size if needed, never remove SL logic.

✕ 7. Risking More to Recover

- Big loss? You increase size to "make it back."
- The market doesn't care. You're emotionally compromised and compounding stupidity.
- *Solution:* Cut the day. Review. Don't trade when tilted.

✕ 8. Following Telegram Gurus or Panic Tweets

- Social media = zero accountability, maximum noise.
- Someone says "Buy XYZ" — but your chart says no.
- You click anyway. You lose.
- *Solution:* One mentor. One system. One trusted bias — **your own**.

✕ 9. Forgetting Position Sizing Rules

- In volatile markets, moves are fast and big.
- 1 wrong oversized trade = wrecked account.
- *Solution:* Stick to 0.5%–1% per trade max. Especially on volatile days.

✕ 10. Letting a Day Turn Into a Spiral

- First trade loss → emotional → second loss → revenge click → wipeout.
- It happens fast.
- *Solution:* Have a daily loss cap. After 2 reds, walk away.

The pros aren't perfect. They just avoid the big mistakes faster than the rest.

🎯

Bonus 4

Printable Mindset Poster

Read this before every session. Then go trade like a sniper.

🧠 THE TRADER'S MINDSET – WALL POSTER

🎯 I TRADE WHEN:

- My mind is clear, not craving
- The setup matches my system — not my mood
- My stoploss and target are defined
- I'm ready to lose and move on
- I've done my prep, not just opened my chart

⚔️ I NEVER:

- Trade out of boredom
- Enter without a stop
- Add to a losing trade
- Move my SL to "give it space"
- Let one red day ruin my process

🧩 I REMEMBER:

- A good trade can still lose
- A bad trade can still win — but that doesn't make it right
- Patience pays more than prediction
- Silence beats noise. Focus beats speed
- I'm here to trade well — not often

🛡 **I AM:**

- A sniper, not a spray shooter
- An executor, not a gambler
- A student of structure, not emotions
- Calm in chaos
- Consistent in process
- Sharp. Clean. Controlled.

No high exists that beats the feeling of a clean trade executed with discipline.

I don't chase candles. I follow process.

I don't fight the market. I flow with it.

I don't trade to feel alive. I trade to grow — quietly, precisely, relentlessly.

✅ **Stick it on your wall. Read it daily. Let it rewire your instinct.**

www.ingramcontent.com/pod-product-compliance
Lightning Source LLC
LaVergne TN
LVHW100318210926
848480LV00003B/1171